A Divine Event

and other

essays

Neville Goddard

Copyright © 2017 Merchant Books

ISBN 978-1-60386-742-9

Contents

A Divine Event

Christmas is the proclamation of a divine event to which all creation aspires. It is an event which puts an entirely different light upon human life, for it proclaims that man has been saved. I question seriously whether an nth part of one per cent of those who call themselves Christians know what this event is about. Tonight, I will tell you from my personal experience.

Paul tells us in his letter to the Corinthians that "No one can say 'Jesus is Lord' except by the Holy Spirit." Now, the Holy Spirit is nothing more than the individual's personal experience of the event, for in the Book of John, the Risen Christ proclaims that he will "send the Comforter, the Holy Spirit, who will lead you into all things and bring to your remembrance all that I have said to you." In the beginning you were told that which seemed incredible, and the Holy Spirit is your experience of that event, for only then can you know that Jesus is Lord.

Now, who is Jesus? He is your awareness, your I AMness. In the Book of Exodus, Moses was told to "Say unto the people of Israel, 'I am has sent you.' This is my name forever. By this name I shall be remembered throughout all generations, and besides me there is no other Lord." Jesus is the Lord, your I AMness; your consciousness of being. "Joshua" is the Hebraic form of our word "Jesus" and means "Jehovah is savior." There is no other Lord than I am. "Our God is a God of salvation. To God, the Lord, belongs escape from death." God is buried in humanity to make man a living being. And he will rise in the individual as his own wonderful human imagination.

The discovery of the God within is the one far–off divine event to which creation moves. The only resurrection spoken of in scripture is when he rises in you, and the only birth spoken of there is when he comes out – and that is Christmas. The event seems to be single and separate from the other events, but they are all part of a complex whole. We are now approaching one part we call Christmas: the birth of God, the birth of I am!

Where could you go that you are not aware of being? Therefore, where can you go and not find God? If you lived in hell would you not be aware of being there? So, God is in hell. If you lived in ecstasy you would be aware of your ecstatic mood, and that awareness is God, for I am is the only name of Jesus.

In his Book called Acts, Luke said: "There is no other name under heaven given among men by which we must be saved." To call Jesus? No! To be aware! Without using words, when you are aware you are saying I am. That is Jesus, who is buried and rises in you. And when he escapes from the tomb of your skull, Christ is born. We are taught that this happened 2,000 years ago among people who are long gone from the world, but I know from experience that when it happens in you it is strangely contemporary. Yes, Christ was born. That is a fact, but it is not over, as it is still taking place in the individual the world over. Christmas is that one far–off great divine event to which the whole vast world is moving.

If you ask someone who calls himself a Christian, who Christ is, the chances are he would tell you that Jesus is the son of God. And if you told him that he must be God to know that, he would be horrified and tell you that you are blasphemous to suggest such a thing. But if you return to the proclamation of the great event, you will find that "No one knows who the son is except the Father." So, if you know God's son is Jesus Christ, then you have to be God the Father. And, since no one knows who the Father is except the son, Jesus Christ must have revealed you as his Father. Well, man cannot rationalize this because he has not had the experience; for no one can know that Jesus is Lord (which is God the Father) except by the Holy Spirit, for it is he who brings you the experience of the great mystery.

We are told that when Paul rose up into the third heaven he heard unutterable words. Some translations say they were "words which man may not utter," but it isn't that. What Paul saw and heard was incapable of expression in words. There are no words to express a body that one wears when he rises within himself, for it is not a body of flesh and blood, but an indescribable form divine. In his 15th chapter of 1 Corinthians, Paul said: "What you sow does not come to life unless it dies. And what you sow is not the body which is to be, for God gives it a body as he has chosen." I will know you in eternity, but for all the identity of purpose there will be a radical discontinuity of form.

Yesterday morning when I returned to this level of my being, I arrested the body I was wearing to spend some ten to fifteen minutes right on the surface of my being. The form is alive. It is all energy, all power, all wisdom, and all love. I wear that body as I do the suit I am wearing now, only I know it to be my very self. I am always in control, by intensifying my energy or modifying it. In that body I looked out over glorious scenes never seen on earth. They were all three–dimensional visions in vivid colors and indescribable forms. I would observe one, then let it go to observe another – all heavenly treasures which are in me.

When your eyes begin to open inwardly into the world of thought, into eternity, you will see what no mortal eye turned out could ever see. There are no images in this outer world to describe the eternal world which is imperishable, the world you will see when you are wearing Christ, the New Man.

This is an indescribable, ineffable, mystery; for God comes to us as one unknown, yet one who will allow the individual to experience who he is. When you experience Christ, you are experiencing who you are, for you are the Jesus of scripture. You are the Lord God Jehovah. The event toward which you are moving is the awakening of the Lord in you. Then and only then will you know who you are.

Christmas is simply the proclamation of this one far–off divine event to which creation moves. It is not about one who lived a long time ago, but about you. The Bible is very personal. It is your own spiritual biography, your salvation history. To see the characters of scripture as characters of history is to see truth tempered to the weakness of the human soul. They are not characters on the outside, but within you, for the drama unfolds in your imagination. You are buried in yourself and do not know it. But when you reach the fullness of time you will awake to Christmas.

Last lecture night I told you of an experience of a friend who tasted of the power of the age to come. She had found herself, in dream, in the home of people who have not changed the fashion of their outer garments for 300 years. The woman's second husband had been killed by the group and she tried to persuade them that what they had done was wrong, but they would not believe her. A group of men all dressed in black and carrying machine guns arrived, ready to kill everyone, and when she tried to persuade them that it was wrong they could not understand. Then she began to awake in her dream to realize that, although they all seemed to be independent of her perception of them, they were only aspects of her dream. Arresting her power of perception, everything froze. She changed their intentions, released the activity in her which allowed them to become reanimated again, and watched as the man put down his gun and with outstretched arms went over to embrace the woman.

This is the power of which I speak. It is a power unknown to the mortal, rational mind. We think power is in the atom bomb, in hydrogen energy, money in the bank, or securities. Tonight, undoubtedly a dozen or more very wealthy men will die and not take one penny with them. They simply left the garment of flesh and blood they made so real, along with their securities. But you can never lose the power of which I speak, for it is forever. These bodies die, and all that they possess will die with them; but the power of imagination is imperishable, for it is the power of God in man, called Christ. Man is slowly awakening to this power and when he hears and senses it, this is the power he will exercise.

Now, in my friend's case, she awoke in her dream to discover that, although everything seemed to be taking place independent of her perception of it, the dream was only herself pushed out. Knowing that she could control the dream, she changed the motivation of the man from murder to love. Then she released the activity which allowed them to become reanimated again, and they obeyed her command. This is your future, your inheritance where everything is under your control.

These bodies of flesh and blood are only garments God wears. Even though they are consumed in a furnace (called cremation), the bodies are restored for others to occupy. The world is restored, but you – the actor in the drama – move up until you finally awake, and that is what we call Christmas.

Christmas is the awakening of God in man. It's not an event which took place 2,000 years ago, but is taking place all over the world in those who have reached the fullness of time. When the fullness of time has come for you, you begin to stir, to awaken from this dream of death and come out of your skull, which is your birth from above. These two events take place the same night. We separate them by three and a half months, and then add a few months to the discovery of the fatherhood of God, then more time to the ascension of the spirit; but there are four parts of the one grand event. The first is resurrection. The second is birth. The third is the discovery of the fatherhood through the son, and the fourth is the ascension: the rising of the son of man (who you are) into heaven in a serpentine form.

Tonight, many are preparing for the great event and singing their heads off on Christmas morning. I'm all for it. Let them have fun. But they will be singing of one they do not know. They will sing their hallelujahs thinking that someone in time and space is responding to their adulation – but that's not Christmas. In the world, moving among them walk those who have experienced the event. They know that Jesus is Lord and that he is their wonderful human imagination, their I AMness.

I am is Jehovah's name forever. By this name I shall be remembered throughout all generations. You are now a living being because Jehovah is buried within you. And you are destined to become a life–giving spirit, as my friend discovered she was. Stopping the activity in herself which allowed others to be alive, she changed their motivation by giving a command which was in conflict with their intentions. Then she released the activity in her and they became reanimated once more – not to carry out their former intention, but to execute her command. She has now tasted of the power of the age to come.

On this level we argue, trying to persuade the other that he is wrong when he knows he is right, so we end up just where we stand. This is life in a world of death where everything waxes, wanes, and vanishes.

But you are destined to enter the world of which I speak. It is eternal and cannot be entered with a body of flesh and blood, but requires a new body. So, unless what you sow dies, it cannot be made alive. And what you sow is not the body which is to be, but God (who is yourself) gives you a body as he has chosen. It is a glorious body of power and wisdom and called the body of Christ. It is worn as you would a garment, only you are in control of your power through your innate wisdom – a wisdom to which no doubt is attached. This proclamation is not discovered by some rational argument. The gospel is not discovered, it is disclosed. It is not something you can logically prove, but a self–revelation of God. Scholars can study the life and teachings of Jesus until the end of time but never find in the study who the Father or the Son is. If they did, they would not tamper with the Bible.

In the earliest of all the books, the Book of Mark, the statement is made: "The beginning of the gospel of Jesus

Christ, the son of God." The phrase, "the son of God," is an addition by a scribe. The earliest and best manuscripts that we have, omit the phrase, "the son of God," and read: "The beginning of the gospel of Jesus Christ."

The word "gospel" means "good news." This is the good news, that Jesus is the Lord Jehovah and Christ is his power and wisdom. He is buried in us and he will rise in us. You will know of his rising because the day he rises in you, the very imagery of scripture will surround you, and you will know that you are the one spoken of as the Lord Jesus Christ. Then you will discover who the son is, for you will not know that Jesus is Lord except by the Holy Spirit (by experience.) And you can only know your son from experience. David, the personification of humanity fused into a single being, stands before you and calls you Father

You are told at the end of the Old Testament that "A son honors his father. If then I am a father, where is my honor?" In other words, where is my son? The New Testament begins by revealing the son, but man cannot understand. He does not know that Jesus is the Lord who is God the Father, until he has the experience of waking and rising in his skull. Of coming out of that skull and holding the Christ child, the sign of his resurrection, in his own hands. He must stand before the son of God and David must call him Father. And may I tell you: at that moment there will be no doubt in his mind as to who the son is and who he is relative to that boy. He will know he is David's father and David will know he is his son.

In the Book of Samuel, we read: "When you lie down with your fathers I will raise up after you your son, who will come forth from your body. I will be his father and he shall be my son." Now we jump to the Book of Revelation, where the Lord is speaking, saying: "I am the root and the offspring of David." I am the root, the cause which is the father. And I am the offspring of my son, David; therefore, I am one with my grandson. All of the members of the human race are fused together into a single being called David. And what comes out of that? David's offspring. If David's root is the Lord, what comes out of David must be one with his root, so I am the root and the offspring. I am the grandfather and the grandson and David is my son. Man matures when he becomes his grandfather, for the grandfather is the Lord.

We are dealing with a mystery. If you think when you read the story of the Old or New Testament that you are going to reach truth by some rational argument, you are searching in vain. The wisest of the wise cannot see it, and because it isn't rational they call it a myth. But I tell you: he gives himself to whomever he will, even the lowliest among men. Those who have all their degrees, honors, money, and reputation are dead but do not know it. I do not condemn them or argue with them, but simply walk by, looking for willing ears to tell my story to, and usually it is to those who are not the scholars of the day. Those who hear my words may not understand them, but locking my message in their hearts, they ponder it; and one day, believing as I hoped they would, it will erupt within them. Then they, too, will know that the Lord Jesus is he who the world calls the God of the universe. They will know it because the Holy Spirit brought to their remembrance all that I have told them.

Let the world go blindly on, as it will. Eternity awaits. It doesn't matter how long it takes. Everyone eventually will come into this knowledge. But no one will come until he hungers, until he thirsts after God with a thirst that only an experience of God can satisfy.

The world, not understanding scripture, thinks that God will send a physical famine. Oh, that is possible, it happens all over the world anyway. It's not because we cannot supply the food – the problem is economic. We are told to curtail production, as we cannot find bins large enough to house our supply. We put an enormous weight on the taxpayer because we allow food to rot, as we do not know how to give it away. People are paid not to grow food, while our government talks about not being able to supply. Our southern states alone could grow enough to feed and clothe the world, but how to do it under the present economy? I am not an economist so I cannot tell you how; but I do know it is not a lack of production, but rather a lack of economy.

The economic problem I cannot solve, but I can tell you that Christ in you is your own wonderful human imagination, that the God of scripture and the Lord Jesus Christ is your I am. Let the world scoff at it. That is perfectly all right; they are only fulfilling scripture. "Scoffers will come scoffing saying, 'Where is the promise of his coming? For ever since the fathers fell asleep, all things have continued as they were from the foundation of the world.'" So, let them scoff, but you accept my message and put your hope fully upon the grace that is coming to you. Hope it will erupt within you now, in the not distant future; and then – when you shed this garment of flesh (as you must), you will be clothed in power; clothed in wisdom; clothed in love.

Those who have not had the experience before they depart this world are restored to life to find themselves in a world just like this. They will be faced with all the problems they have neglected here. They may leave the garment of a billionaire to find themselves a shoeshine boy or one who cleans latrines, if that is what must be done to rouse them to believe the incredible story.

Don't think that your present position in life is any indicator of what you will be when you leave here. If Christ has not awakened in you, you will find yourself in a terrestrial world like this, in a body like these, new and young, but not a baby. You will be doing something best suited for the work yet to be done in you. Until that power in you awakes, you will continue using your rational mind in a rational world just like this.

The Christmas that we now look forward to celebrate is one aspect of the great event. There are four definite acts in the single event, which begin with your resurrection. This is followed by your birth from above. Then David reveals your fatherhood, and the fourth and final act appears when you ascend into heaven in a serpentine form and enter it violently, clothed in power.

Now let us go into the silence.

A Lesson *in* Scripture

In the second chapter of the Book of Luke the story is told of Jesus' parents, worried and seeking him for three days, finding him and complaining, to which Jesus said: "How is it that you sought me? Know you not that I must be about my Father's business?" I ask you not to put yourself in that frame of mind. Your earthly parents seek you and, at the tender age of twelve, you dare to say to them: "I must be about my Father's business."

This statement has reference to the 40th Psalm and the 4th chapter of John. In the 40th Psalm you are told: "In the role of the book it is written about me." Every man is destined to discover that scripture is his autobiography. It's not written about individual beings like Jesus Christ, Moses, Abraham, Isaac, Jacob, and so on who lived unnumbered years ago, but about the individual you! The 4th chapter of the Book of John begins with a discussion between the Lord Jesus Christ and a woman of Samaria about a well and water. After this discussion the disciples say to Jesus: "Master you have had nothing to eat" and he replies: "I have food you know not of. My food is to do the will of him who sent me and to finish his work."

This is true. You have come into this world only to finish the work of him who sent you. And who is he? The Father. "He who sees me, sees he who sent me. I came out from the Father and came into the world. Again, I leave the world and return to the Father. He who sees me sees the Father, for I and the Father are one."

Conceiving the thought in the beginning, God had to have an agent to express it. Everything in this world needs man to express it and may I tell you: God is man. In the beginning God made man in his image. "Male/female made he them and called their name Man." Read it carefully in the 5th chapter of Genesis. Creating Man to express himself, God comes into the world to express and finish what he conceived in the beginning. Conceiving a state and knowing it takes a man to express it; God sent himself from the depth of his own being into this world to fulfill the state.

"In the beginning was the Word (the purpose) and the Word was with God and the Word was God." The Old Testament is God's Word (his plan) which he made known through his servants, the prophets. The New Testament interprets the Old. The story of Jesus Christ is the interpretation of the prophecy recorded in the Old. Read it carefully, for everything said of Jesus Christ, you are going to experience. It is said: "His name shall be called the Word of God." Called God's Word, his seed, his creative power, your imagination is God's creative power and wisdom. Can you conceive of any greater wisdom than your own wonderful human imagination? Think of something. The moment you do, it's right before your mind's eye. Maybe you can't draw a straight line, yet you can imagine your mother even though she is gone from this world. Think of anyone and they instantly appear before your mind's eye. That is your own wonderful creative power–filled imagination who is Jesus Christ in you. It is he who has come into the world to fulfill the Word of God, and everything must be fulfilled by the Jesus Christ in you, who is your hope of glory.

We are told in the 22nd chapter of the Book of Luke: "Scripture must be fulfilled in me," so you must be about your Father's business by experiencing everything said of Jesus Christ in scripture. The miraculous birth will be yours, the discovery of the Fatherhood, the ascent into heaven and the descent of the Holy Spirit upon you in the bodily form of a dove. Then like the psalmist you will say: "Thou hast delivered me from the world of death," for you will know from experience that in the volume of the book it was all about you!

I have been sent from the depth of my soul to act as a magnet to those who are about to fulfill scripture, and they come, each in his own order. Last Friday morning my friend Bennie found himself cataleptic. Unable to open his eyes or move his body, Ben could hear within himself the cry of a child as he felt an unearthly wind in his skull. Then a star exploded from his skull and a child wrapped in swaddling clothes fell into his arms. Looking at the child he said: "Oh, my darling" and knew that no one in eternity could care for that child but himself. As the vision faded he was given a photograph of the child.

The birth from above came to Bennie that way. He was left with a photograph. This happened on the 20th day of October. Now, if the current record of order is correct (and it has happened to my friend Bob and myself), five months from now Bennie will experience the coming of God's only Son, David, who will reveal him as the Father. I am basing my interpretation from what he told me, and I say the birth has happened to him. Why should the birth occur in the same manner to any two when God is infinite in his creation? Of all the children who come into the world, seemingly from the womb of woman, no two births are exactly alike, there is always something different.

Only a couple of days before this happened to Bennie, he said:, "In the spirit you were teaching the word of God when someone said: 'Tell us the story of Jesus' and you replied: 'The story of Jesus is a persistent assumption that you are what you want to be, that things are as you desire them to be.'" This is true, for unless you believe that you are the being you now worship on the outside, you remain desiring and die in your sins of unfulfilled desires. You've got to begin to believe that you are Jesus Christ, the Word of God, which – having gone out will not return empty, but will fulfill your purpose and accomplish that which you sent yourself to do. What is that? To fulfill scripture. That's all you are here for.

On this level you can be rich if that is your desire, but remember the story of Jesus is persistent assumption. You can persist in the assumption that you are wealthy. I have many friends across this country who are very, very wealthy, yet I would say ninety–nine percent of them are miserable; but they will all tell you the same thing. I think of one in particular now. She has a fortune in diamonds. Tiffany, who sells diamonds marked up 300–400%, offered her $100,000 for one piece. When she joins us for dinner in New York City she wears a broach, a ring, and a pendant, worth a half million dollars. Ruth was born a very poor girl and – desiring wealth – she persistently assumed she was married to tremendous wealth. She had no money. Her only claim to any social status was that she was a descendant of the Adams who were in the White House. He, on the other hand, came out of a line of rascals. His great–grandfather was a bishop in New York; therefore, had good advice as to his descent and how to guard it. Ruth married and lived in hell for twenty–odd years, bearing him three sons. Now well into her seventies, her only desire is to marry more wealth and have more diamonds.

That is all right. The story of Jesus is a complete and undeviating persistence in the assumption that you are what you want to be. If you haven't experienced wealth and that is what you want, persistently assume "I am wealthy." If you have not experienced fame, assume you are famous, but "The day will come," saith the Lord "when I will send a famine upon you. It will not be a hunger for bread or a thirst for water, but for the hearing of my Word." If that hunger hasn't come to you, then take the same story of Jesus and fulfill your every desire.

When I am in New York, my friend comes to every meeting. She is a delightful person, but she is brutally honest with her desires. She wants more and more diamonds, more emeralds, more museum pieces. She confessed that she had no hunger to hear anything about David, but wants more and more money to leave her two sons. She wants more and more worldly illusions; but it is my hope that the hunger has come to you who are here – not for more and more bread and water, but for hearing the word of God with understanding.

The Book of Luke begins: "I have come to fulfill scripture. Then beginning with Moses in the law and the prophets and the psalms, he interpreted to them in all the scriptures the things concerning himself." Questioning his earthly parents, he asks: "Why do you seek me? Do you not know that I must be about my Father's business?" . . . fulfilling scripture? Entering the temple, he is given a book which he opens and reads the first verse and half of the second of the 61st chapter of Isaiah, saying: "The Spirit of the Lord is upon me, for he has anointed me to preach glad tidings to the poor and suffering. To open the prison doors to all who are in prison."

Now, claiming to have come only to fulfill scripture, he tells you that the Spirit of the Lord God was upon him that day. It is not expressed that way in Luke, but he says – as you heard it "this day" – it was fulfilled. What does he mean? That he saw the Spirit descend in bodily form as a dove. It has been fulfilled in him and he is urging everyone to follow his pattern, for no one comes to the Father save by this pattern. The Spirit of the Lord God descended in bodily form as a dove. The same dove who returned to Noah in the ark. Man is the ark of God and the dove – coming to bring assurance that everything is all right – descends upon one, and as it remains he is told to "Rise and anoint him, for this is he." Luke tells you how he is fulfilling scripture, for he knows that "In the volume of the book it is all about me."

Like Paul, I have not restrained my lips. I have told of your deliverance. I have told of your everlasting love to anyone and everyone who will listen. They may not accept my words, but I do know that within a certain group the hunger is there and they will all begin to awake.

Now, in the 30th chapter of the Book of Jeremiah, the Lord speaks, saying: "Can a man bear a child? Why then do I see every man with his hands pulling himself out of himself like a woman in labor." The Hebrew word "chalatz" (translated in both the King James Version and the Revised Standard Version as "loins") means "to take off; to pull oneself out of oneself; to deliver." When the Psalmist said: "He has delivered my soul from death" he was speaking of the physical body. It is a garment of death which appears in the world, waxes, wanes, vanishes, and turns into dust. The word translated "delivered" in the Psalms, is the same word which was translated "loins" in Jeremiah.

So, can a Man bear a child? Yes. Let us go back to what I quoted earlier. "Male/female made he them and called their name Man." There is a womb in the male/female unlike that of an earthly woman. This womb is the skull of generic Man. It is there that God has planted His Word which cannot return unto him void, but must accomplish that which is His purpose and prosper in the thing for which he sent it. That purpose is to fulfill scripture, for God has an entirely different world awaiting those who fulfill His Word.

We are told: "This Word is truth." Everyone enters the world to fulfill the truth and will not depart until God's Word is accomplished. If God's Word has not been fulfilled in you when the world calls you dead, you are restored to a life just as real as this, in a world just as real as this, to continue your journey until the hunger comes upon you and you will be drawn to that final point.

In his book called Urizen, William Blake tells of the serpent in the womb of Enitharmon who, shredding the scales of death, his hissing changes into the cry of a child and

> *"The dead heard the voice of the child*
> *And began to awake from sleep*
> *All things heard the voice of the child*
> *And began to awake to life."*

You actually hear the cry of the child in your skull. It seems impossible, but may I tell you: it is true.

Now, to encourage those who are not interested in that aspect of the truth, let me go back to what Bennie heard me say in the spirit: "The story of Jesus is a persistent assumption." This is true in every aspect of your life. You want to be rich? That's the story of Jesus, which is a persistent assumption in the conviction that "I am rich," for unless you believe that "I am rich" you die in your sins and continue to claim "I am poor." You want to be known? Then persistently assume: "I am known." Want to be healthy? "I am healthy!" Regardless of what you want to be, you must declare you already are it and persist in that assumption. An assumption is an act of faith, and without faith it is impossible to please God. Your reasoning mind may deny wealth. Your senses deny it too, but if you have faith you will dare to assume wealth, thereby becoming the man you want to be.

Maybe, tonight you would rather continue to worship a Jesus Christ on the outside. Maybe you would rather continue to walk with the sheep of the world and not be the shepherd, but you would like to feed on green pastures by still waters, instead of climbing the steep hills of doubt and fear as most people do. You can, if you will persistently assume: "I am well fed. I am wanted. I am known and everything is as I want it to be." But remember: to bring all these things into being, there must be a persistent assumption. That's the story of Jesus.

Now we are told in Jeremiah that God's word will not turn back until he has executed and accomplished the intents of his mind, which is that you become God. "In the later days you will understand it clearly." It is God's purpose to give himself to man and he will not turn back until he has executed and accomplished the intents of his mind. So, in the final days he sends a hunger unto your heart – not for bread, a larger home or jewelry – but for the hearing of the Word of God. When this hunger possesses you, nothing will satisfy you but an experience of God. And if it is God's purpose to give you himself as himself, when you have experienced his Word you are God!

Here is the story: "What is the greatest commandment, master? "Hear O Israel: The Lord our God, the Lord is one." In the original manuscript the word "hear" is "shema" whose last letter is larger than the other letters in the word. This is also true of the world "echad" (translated "one") at the end of the sentence. Put the two words together and they spell a word meaning "witness."

At the very end of the Book of Luke you read: "You are witnesses of these things, but remain here until you are endowed with power from on high." What power? The power of God called Jesus Christ. You are destined to put on and wear the Lord Christ Jesus as you would a garment. Wait for it, for it will be born within you. And when God's power and wisdom is born, you will find the sign of his birth in the form of a little child. Then all of these signs will unfold in you and you will wear the garment of Jesus Christ. So, I tell you, you will be witnesses of all that I have told you, for now I am returning to the very source out of which I came.

I came into the world completely forgetful of the being that I AM. I had to. When I first met my friend Abdullah back in 1931 I entered a room where he was speaking and when the speech was ended he came over, extended his hand and said: "Neville, you are six months late." I had never seen the man before, so I said: "I am six months late? How do you know me?" and he replied: "The brothers told me that you were coming and you are six months late."

I was late because the one who told me of Abdullah was a Catholic priest. I loved him dearly, but I thought he was almost a moron. His father, a rumrunner in the days of prohibition, left him two million dollars, which he proceeded to lose on Wall Street the first year. The only wonderful thing he did was to take the last $15,000 and give it to a Catholic organization to care for his mother the rest of her earthly days. So, having no respect for his judgment, when he told me about Abdullah I postponed going to hear him until one day I could find no excuse. When Ab called me by name I said: "I don't know you" and he replied: "Oh yes you do, but you have forgotten. We were together in China thousands of years ago, but you promised to completely forget in order to play the part you must play now."

Last Friday night a lady gave me a letter saying: "The previous Monday as you stood on the platform I could not see you as Neville, but as an ancient Chinese philosopher. I have seen my friends change from moment to moment, but you remained changed during your entire lecture. This bothered me, so I questioned the experience on the way home and then I remembered. Several years ago, in a psychic experience, I was walking up a hill with other students to attend a class. Falling away from the group, I saw an ancient Chinese in a white garment at my side. Beckoning me to follow him, we approached a cave where I saw huge granite stone with a peak at the top. Two hands containing a cocoon covered the top of the stone. Removing the cocoon, the ancient Chinese broke it on the peak of the granite, and water, mixed with colorful oil, came out as life took on the sense of heat rising. Then the ancient Chinese took my hand and led me back to the group, where they had not realized that I had been away. "Now I know whose face you wore last Monday night."

Well, that's what Abdullah told me in 1931, but to this day I have no knowledge of it, because I swore in the beginning to empty myself completely of all memory and take on the form of a slave, but to have faith in him who sent me. Now knowing that he and I are one, I have no other place to go but back to myself, the sender. Having played every part, I have completely wiped out the memory, but I know that no one can arrive at the end of the road until he has played it all. I do know from my intuitive knowledge that, just as an actor must feel the part he is playing and imagine himself the character he is depicting, you will imagine yourself into every part, and when the play is over for you, the signs will come to show you the being that you really are.

You who are here are hungry for the Word of God. You are thirsty for the Word of God. You could be at home this night watching TV and it would cost you nothing, but you have given up your time and your money to be here because of your hunger. I have been sent to tell you not only that you become God when he is fulfilled in you, but how to cushion the blows in this world of reason by delighting in his law. His law is simply a persistent assumption in the claim: "I am what I want to be." Do not judge one who does not have the hunger for the Word of God, but tell him how to become what he wants to be.

Tell him that the story of Jesus is a perpetual, persistent assumption in whatever he wants to be. That Christ in him is the power of God and his imagination is that power and wisdom. Tell him that imagination knows how to bring his assumption to pass, but that he must persist.

Now I ask you: are you willing to persist in the assumption that you are what you want to be? Or are you going to go home tonight and say: "That was a nice little talk he gave, but after all he has a million dollars in the bank and I have nothing." If you think that, you are disobedient, for by that thought you have lack of faith in "I am he!" That's the fundamental sin of the universe. There are only two sins recorded in scripture that offend God. One is: "Unless you believe that I am he you die in your sins," and the other is eating of the fruit of tree of knowledge of good and evil. Ask our generals tonight if it would be good to stop bombing Vietnam and they would say No. Go across the ocean and ask the Vietnamese and they would say Yes – so what is good and what is evil?

I am not asking anyone but you! What would be good for you? Tell me, because in the end every conflict will resolve itself as the world is simply mirroring the being you are assuming that you are. One day you will be so saturated with wealth, so saturated with power in the world of Caesar, you will turn your back on it all and go in search for the Word of God. I remember when I had so much wealth. I did not have one home, but many, each fully staffed from secretaries to gardeners. That was a life of sheer decadence. I recall walking out of it and not returning. Whether they ever found the body I do not know, but I do know I deliberately walked away. Then about ten years ago in one of my journeys in spirit, I walked back into the world and saw it just as it was before. Strangely enough, everyone recognized me and welcomed me with open arms, but I stayed only for a moment then returned here bringing with me its vivid memory. So, I do believe that one must completely saturate himself with the things of Caesar before he is hungry for the Word of God.

I am convinced you are here because of your hunger. I know you have obligations to society, you must pay Caesar's debts, so you want more money, but your hunger is greater for the hearing of the Word of God than for things of Caesar. That is why you are here, and you are blessed by it.

Now let us go into the silence.

A Movement *of* Mind

In the 33rd chapter of the Book of Job we are told that God speaks to man in two ways, but man does not perceive them. It is said: "In a dream, in a vision of the night when deep sleep falls upon men while they slumber on their beds, he opens the ears of men and seals their instructions." Tell that to a psychiatrist and, because he separates the dreamer from God, he will tell you that all dreams come from the individual dreamer and not from God. But I tell you: God's eternal name is I AM, and if I asked who is dreaming the dream would the individual not say, "I am?" And are we not told that that is God's name forever and ever?

You cannot separate the dreamer from God, and all dreams proceed from Him. Some are simple and need no interpretation, while others are revealed in a symbolic language and need an interpreter, as told us in the story of Joseph. His true identity is revealed when he looked into the faces of those who had had a dream and saw they were disturbed, for he said: "Do not interpretations belong to God? Tell me your dream." Then he interpreted the dreams of the butler, the baker, and even Pharaoh himself, and they all came to pass just as he had said they would. Now, if only God can interpret a dream, why tell Joseph? Because he is a personification of God. His name was changed from Joseph (meaning "salvation") to Joshua, which means "Jehovah is salvation."

Now back in 1954, I awoke from a dream hearing these words: "You do not move in waking any more than you move on your bed in sleep. It is all a movement of mind. The intensity is determined by the strength of the vortex you create, which is just like a whirlwind with a center of perfect stillness. You only believe that you are moving when you are awake, as you think you move in sleep." Well, I am a rational being and reason could not accept that statement, but I wrote it down and placed it in my Bible to await further revelation.

Psychiatrists would say this message came from myself. I will not deny that, but I do know that it came from a depth of my own being which my rational mind does not reach. Today our three astronauts returned from a trip of half a million miles. You and I came here tonight in our cars, and throughout my lifetime I have traveled all over the world in ships and planes. And like Blake, in my dreams "I have traveled through a land of men, a land of men and women, too. And heard and seen such dreadful things as cold earth wanderers never knew." We have all traveled, yet I know what I heard and wrote down. I know that I have traveled in my dreams and yet I know I have not physically left my room, for when I awoke in the morning I was still on the bed upon which I fell asleep. So, I ask you: is this waking state no more than a dream? Is there a dreamer in the depths of my being who looks upon this world as a dream, just as I who – having gone to a little lower of the dream at night – awake to find I haven't left my bed at dawn?

Paul tells us that "We are born anew through the resurrection of Jesus Christ from the dead." I remember that night, for I felt myself waking from a deep, deep sleep, feeling a vibration which, although centered in my head, it seemed to be coming from without. Then I awoke within the sepulcher – the skull – in which I was buried, to come out to find all of the symbolism of the Christian mystery surrounding me. I saw the infant wrapped in swaddling clothes and the three witnesses to the event. Although unseen, as I was spirit, the witnesses spoke of me as the father of the child – the sign that my savior was born, fulfilling scripture: "This shall be a sign unto you, you shall find a child wrapped in swaddling clothes, lying in a manger."

That night I awoke from a far deeper level of my being to find the symbolism of my waking from the dream of life, just as day after day I wake from the dream of the night. So, could it be that the revelation I heard back in 1954 is literally true? Reason questions it, reason doubts it, and reason rejects it. So, if the vision is true then reason is rejecting Jesus Christ, for Jesus Christ defines himself as the truth, saying: "I am the truth..." If the revelation is true, and reason rejects it, is not reason Satan, the doubting one?

This statement cannot be logically proved. Its truth must be experienced. I had completely forgotten it until I discovered my note today while looking in my Interpreter's Bible, and there it was – the note I wrote on the 28th day of November 1954: "You do not move in waking any more than you move on your bed in sleep. It is all a movement of mind. The intensity is determined by the strength of the vortex you create, which is just like a whirlwind with a center of perfect stillness. You only believe that you are moving when you are awake, as you think you move in sleep."

Scripture speaks of two ages: this age of darkness and decay, and that age of light and eternal life. This age is one of motion and violence, turbulence and storms, as the dreamer in men is sound asleep and does not know that he is God. In the 44th Psalm, however, he is urged to "Rouse thyself, why sleepest thou, O Lord. Awake! Do not cast us off forever."

While occupying his dream God has the sensation of travel, motion and violence; but when he awakes he will find himself in the sepulcher, the skull of Man, where he deliberately laid himself down to sleep and was buried. God crucified himself on the cross of man and is dreaming this dream of life so that man may become God.

Now I want to clarify a few points. In the Book of John this statement is made: "His voice you have never heard, his form you have never seen, neither does his word abide in you because you do not believe him whom he has sent." Many of you have completely accepted the fact that I have been sent. You believe me when I tell you that I stood in the presence of the Risen Lord, who embraced me and I became one with. Having been incorporated into the body of Love, Almighty God sent me to tell my experience. Having accepted my words, many of you have had a sexual experience with me, in vision, and have interpreted this to be a physical experience on this level; but it is not, as this is a shadow world. Your acceptance brought about this union, yet I – the speaker – am totally unaware of it. The true story of Christ which I have brought you has now been made alive in you. It will erupt in time and your experience of scripture will be identical to mine.

The males who have completely accepted my words will not experience a sexual act, but an embrace. Wearing the body of the Risen Lord, who is Infinite Love and with whom I am now one, you will see my face. You will be asked to name the greatest thing in the world and, as though divinely inspired, you will quote the words of Paul saying: "Faith, hope, and love; these three, but the greatest of these is love." I will embrace you, and you will fuse with the one body of the Risen

Lord, and he who is united with the Lord becomes one Spirit with him.

All of these are symbols, telling you that, having believed him whom he sent, you will hear his voice and see his form as his word is now abiding in you. It's a complete break with the past, as told us in the first words the Risen Lord spoke in the Book of Mark: "Repent and believe in the gospel." The gospel is the good news that man is not lost; that scripture is not secular history, but divine history, which was plotted and planned before we came out from the Father and came into the world to enter our own creation and play all the parts.

It is God who awakes in you. One man, containing all, fell into diversity as told us in the 82nd Psalm: "I say, 'You are gods, sons of the Most High, all of you; nevertheless, you shall die like men, and fall as one man, O princes.'" (I have quoted the Revised Standard Version in the marginal setup which is the true translation of the Hebrew.) It takes all the sons who fell, to form God the Father; so, we are gathered together one by one into that same body which fell into humanity. And from humanity, God extracts himself individually because we are all so unique. No one can be duplicated or lost, because God is buried in all and God is redeeming himself.

Today I watched the exciting touchdown of the astronauts who had traveled to the moon and back. Then I reread what I had written back in 1954: "You do not move in waking any more than you do on your bed in sleep." Now, reason could not accept that statement. I saw the astronauts return. We have a record of their journey of a half–million miles, yet they did not move? Well, I must confess that I have traveled in my dreams, as I am sure you have; yet we always wake on our bed in the morning, do we not? Could there be a dreamer far deeper than the one who is dreaming this seeming waking state? And when he awakes from the dream of life, would he not look upon it as you look upon the dream of the night?

I know that when I awoke from within, I realized that I had been there for unnumbered centuries, dreaming violence, love, hate, concupiscence, and pain – dreaming everything to be real, just as I did in any dream. I awoke to discover that I had been in that skull for centuries, dreaming I was a man walking the earth, dying, being restored to life to die again. This I continued to do until that moment in time when I awoke in Golgotha, the sepulcher where I was buried in the beginning of time. That's my Calvary.

I seem to move here. I get up and shave in the morning, bathe, eat, make an effort to earn a dollar to pay the rent, and do all sorts of things; yet it's all a dream, a dream with a purpose. God limited himself to the limit of contraction and opacity called man and began to dream this world into being. Now believing himself to be you, you can dream noble dreams or ignoble ones. I urge you to dream noble dreams, because when you know you are the dreamer you can make all of your dreams come true.

A dream is a very fluid state. Knowing what you want to dream, bring your inner circle of friends before your mind's eye and allow them to see you as you want to be seen. When you are self–persuaded this is now a fact, relax in the vision's gestation period. There is an interval of time between impregnation and birth. Having seen the expressions on their faces and heard the sound of their voices, break the spell and wait for that impregnation to take place in the world of dreams, while you live in the world of Caesar awaiting its coming.

I have told you that the story of Jesus Christ has unfolded itself within me. What I shared with you tonight is not recorded in scripture; but in the very last verse of the 21st chapter of John he makes this statement: "Many other things Jesus did which are not recorded here. Were every one of them to be written, the world itself could not contain the books." There was no need to record the words which were revealed to me; so, it does fit in with the very last verse of the epilogue of John, for John ends on the 20th verse and the 21st is the epilogue. All of these things happened and many more, but only these were recorded that you may believe.

Thank you for sharing your visions with me, as they are showing me that you have completely accepted the story as I have told it. I have shared with you the true story of Jesus Christ. Over the centuries, barnacles have gathered around the ship. Men, in the interest of their own doctrines, have added to the scriptures. In spite of the warning not to add to or take from the words of the prophecies of the Bible, men have added to, to support their own traditions and conventions. When the original text was written, the one who had the vision simply recorded it. He did not understand it, but wrote it down, as I did, knowing that a greater revelation would come.

I could not understand what I heard in 1954; but in 1959 I knew its truth, for I awoke from a profound dream to discover that I was not on my bed, but in my skull and completely alone. I came out of my skull to find the babe wrapped in swaddling clothes and the witnesses to the event. Seeing the babe, they witnessed the sign of my spiritual birth, but they could not see me as having been born of the spirit. I am Spirit, while they, not yet born of the spirit, are flesh. I didn't bring forth a little baby; the child is but a sign that God is born.

Having begotten himself, he brings forth that which he buried in humanity, for God is redeeming himself, as there is only God in the universe.

The Bible hasn't a thing to do with any morals as the pulpits teach. It makes no attempt to change the world, as it is a schoolhouse. You don't turn a schoolroom into a home. This is a school of educated darkness, where we travel towards the light. Scripture does not attempt to change things; rather it urges all to "Render unto Caesar the things that are Caesar's."

To try to make this world a nice, sweet little place in which all are happy and have enough to eat and drink is fine, but that hasn't a thing to do with the mystery of Christ. Were there no struggle, no effort would be made to awaken from the dream of life. Rather, the sleeper would fall deeper into sleep. So, let them march along telling the world how to become good and kind. It's all nonsense, for as long as man wears the garment of the animal he must express it. Taking from himself the heart and mind of Love, God took upon himself the body, heart, and mind of the animal, as told us in the 4th chapter of Daniel. This is an animal world, but while in this world of violence Jesus Christ awakes to discover it was only a dream. Were it not that Jesus Christ was in you, you could not breathe, for your very breath is his life.

The day will come when you will awake to know this to be true; for David, the sum total of all of the experiences you have had in your dream of being man, will stand before you and call you "Father". Then you will fulfill the 89th Psalm knowing, "I have found David. He has cried unto me, 'Thou art my Father, my God and the Rock of my salvation.' "Having played all the parts of Man, humanity, fused into a single youth, reveals your Godhood.

As the Father, you will know that your son has always done your will; for you will have found in David, the son of Jesse (I AM) one who has done all your will. You, the Father, dreamed it and you, the son. played all the parts. And when the play is over you awake to come out of Golgotha to be born from above. Peter tells us: "We are born anew through the resurrection of Jesus Christ from the dead." While the world worships him as someone coming from without, you will find him rising from within – not as another, but as your very Self, the dreamer of life.

The great poet, Shelley, saw it so clearly when he said: "He has awakened from the dream of life. 'Tis we who, lost in stormy visions, keep with phantoms an unprofitable strife." That's what the world is doing, fighting self–created phantoms. The world is yourself pushed out and you are in conflict with yourself until that day when an unearthly wind possesses you and you awake in your skull with the consuming desire to get out. With your innate knowledge, you will push the base of your skull and something will move. Then you will come out just as a child comes out of the womb of a woman; but this time you are being born, not from below, but from above –from the skull of Self. The word "anothin" is translated "from above." When Pilate said: "Do you not know that I have the power to crucify you or the power to set you free," the Risen Lord replied: "You have no power over me unless it were given to you from above." Here is the same word "anothin." The power to kill or make alive comes from within.

Everything is taking place from within. Having fallen into a profound sleep, you are the Lord Jesus Christ, dreaming the dream of life. And because there is only one Being, everyone will awaken as Jesus, for everything else will vanish and leave

Jesus only. And no one can say that Jesus is Lord except by the Holy Wind. When that wind possesses you, you awake within yourself. Only then will you know you are the Lord Jesus Christ.

Now let us go into the silence.

A Movement Within God

If you find yourself miserable or helpless here, may I tell you that you are not condemned to the state by a deity outside of yourself, for everything that takes place in your world is but a movement within God.

We are told that in the very beginning the Spirit of God moved upon the face of the waters and things came into being. Everything – your misery, your helplessness, your joy, your sorrow – no matter what it is, comes into being by a movement within God, and he is not a deity outside yourself. You are not a helpless being, but the operant power of God. Seated as you are now, you can move without moving physically because your eternal body is all Imagination. Called Jesus Christ in scripture, you are God's power and wisdom. So, if you find yourself in a place where you are miserable and feel helpless, it is because you either knowingly or unknowingly fell into that state, and not because of the condemnation of some deity outside of you.

Every conceivable situation that you could ever think of exists now as a fact in God but cannot be made visible to you until you occupy it, for you are God's operant power. Everything in this world needs man as the agent to express it. Hate or love, joy or sorrow, all things require man to express it. We glorify or condemn the man, but he simply represents a state which God entered knowingly or unknowingly and remained there until the state was externalized. Everyone is free to choose the state he wishes to occupy. You imagined yourself into your present state. If you don't like it, you must imagine yourself out of it and into another. It is all a matter of movement.

We are told that "He chose us in him before the foundation of the world." Collectively forming one glorious being, we conceived a play and speaking as one being, we said: "It is time for the play to begin." Then individually we said: "I AM," and the play began. We conceived a play containing every horrible thing as well as every lovely thing in the world. Every problem and its solution were conceived. In fact, you cannot think of something that was not in that original conception. Then it was time to start, and saying simply: "I AM," God took upon himself that which He had conceived, and your journey into this fabulous world began. So, no matter what you are experiencing now, you are not condemned by some being outside of yourself, for you either wittingly or unwittingly fell into the state, be it good, bad, or indifferent. Now, how to move?

We are told in the very beginning of Genesis that "The Spirit of God moved upon the face of the waters." And in the Book of Joshua (which is the Hebraic name for Jesus) the Lord said: "Wherever the sole of your foot will tread upon, I have given you." Now, you can choose where you want the sole of your foot to tread, for the world is yours and all within it; but remember: whatever you tread upon will be given you!

When I speak of Joshua or Jesus, I am not speaking of any historical creature, but the Christ in you who is the hope of glory! I am trying to get you to realize that Jesus Christ is in you as your own wonderful human imagination. So, when I say: "God became Man that Man may become God" I mean: "Imagination became you that you may become all Imagination." Man has difficulty associating Imagination with

God. Somehow the word "God" denotes some being that created the world, yet remained apart from it, but when I use the word "Imagination" it is my hope that the separation ceases to be. May I tell you: the whole vast world is all imagination. Our realists think they are nearer to the truth, yet they do not realize they are dictating nothing more than their imagination. They laugh at those who are mystically inclined, but may I tell you: leave them alone and go your way in confidence that what you are imagining you already are, you will become.

You imagined yourself into the state you are now occupying, and you can imagine yourself into any state you desire to express. No outside deity moved you into the state of misery you are now expressing; you did it yourself because you forgot who you are. You are the being who conceived every state in the beginning and deliberately started your journey by moving into a state, for you are Jesus, the Lord.

When I speak of Jesus, I am not speaking of some holy person as the world calls holy. The true story of Jesus is not as the churches teach. Their teaching is as far removed from the truth as Dante's "Inferno" is from The Sermon on the Mount. Dante had the capacity to spin beautiful worlds together, but what a state he fell into when he wrote his words. He was supposedly writing scripture and that is what the churches follow, yet it is so completely different from the real, true story of Christ.

Jesus is the very being of everyone in the world. The word "Jesus" means "Jehovah saves," and there is only one savior. Jesus is He who fell and He who saves himself. No one else saves you. You are saved by your own being. Becoming aware, you begin to remember; and remembering, you turn around and come out of the very play in which you sent yourself. And in the end, all are united to form once again the single being that fell. The Lord God Jehovah, containing all, fell into diversity. In the end not one will be lost, but all will be gathered into the unity that is the Lord Jesus Christ. That is the story.

This week I received some beautiful letters. One was from a lady who said: "I heard you ten years ago and shortly after hearing your message I found myself in vision on top of the highest mountain in the universe. I was looking towards the horizon into a fantastic vastness without a shore. Clouds were below me, but as I looked into the distance I saw a little flicker of light, then a spark, and then others. As I watched the flickering lights round about me, I noticed that the cloud below me was making an imperceptible forward motion. Then a burst of white light came through the clouds and filled infinity. The clouds began to disburse, and pointing to the light, I said: "That's Paul." Then the light diffused and a burst of light appeared in living colors, and, pointing to it, I said: "That is Neville." Then came a shower of golden needles which penetrated my brain, and I awoke to write it down. For years I have contemplated this vision, not understanding its meaning until last Monday night, when you spoke of the being of light who shoots his fiery arrows into the brains of those who are called."

May I tell you: it's the same story over and over again. You are the only Christ, the only Lord, the Only God and Father of all! Having conceived the play, you are playing every part and each in his own wonderful time will play the part of Jesus Christ, for in the end we will all know that we are God. Then you will hate no one, for you will realize that we agreed to play all the parts while hiding behind the masks we wear. Now completely masked, we think we are many and do not recognize ourselves as the one who conceived and predicted the play of life.

You are not now in a fatalistic state. You fell into the state because it was arranged in the beginning that you could fall into and move out of every state. So, keep on going and complete the play, for when the play is finished, you turn around and return to the very being you were in the beginning!

Now, a gentleman wrote, saying: "I saw a man, about 26 years of age. He had golden curls on his head and seemed to be sunk into the ground. Two men appeared to be working on the top of his head towards the back of his skull. As I watched the young man raised his arm, and touching his head he put his hand into his skull. Curious, I came closer to see an enormous skull made of clay or some form of plastic, which was completely empty. Moving to look at the front of the man, the scene changed, and now I see his chin resting on the sands of the desert. The mask looked like those shown in Africa or Hawaii, where you only see the mask but never the wearer. I knew I was seeing a mask, but its wearer was unseen."

That is the world! You don't know it, but when you are looking at a seeming other you are seeing an intimate being, one you knew in the beginning, one you will remember when all of the masks are removed – for we are all wearing masks in order to play this play called life. In this world Imagination plays the role of the weak man, the strong man, the poor man and the rich man, for the roles were conceived in the beginning by Imagination, and Imagination is playing all the parts.

You, imagining, are God – who is all Imagination. That's all there is. The universe is nothing more than Imagination creating while it is fast asleep! You and I move from state to state, either deliberately (by knowing what we are doing), or unintentionally (by falling into a state as we read the headlines of the paper). Listen to the radio or watch TV tonight, and although you may know none of the facts, if you accept what is said you will fall into a state and buy things you do not need. You will fill your house with all kinds of trivia that you have no room for because Imaginations is operating! Someone conceived a plan to get you to empty your pockets and buy their products, and you will, because Imagination is sound asleep. And Imagination will continue the journey until you turn around and head for home by becoming more and more awake!

Those who think they are so very wise in this world know nothing about Jesus. Only the seers, the mystics, know who He is. Only those who have seen the light he claims he is and know his form without seeing the face, know him. There are not thousands of lights, but only one vast, infinite light. If one takes on a white light and another multi–colored lights, it's still the same wonderful light of Jesus only. There is only God who is playing all the parts, and in the end, you will know that you are light, that you are Spirit, that you are God, from personal experience.

But tonight, as you sit here, you can mentally shut out the facts of life and move anywhere in your imagination. Do that and no one looking at you physically can tell where you have mentally moved. And if you dwell in imagination where you would like to be, and see what you would see were you there, you will have moved within your own being. Persist and everything here will die because of your move within God.

In the beginning, the Spirit of God moved upon the face of the waters, saying: "Wherever you go and stand, I will give you." You were given everything in the beginning, and one day – having finished the play – you will begin to awaken. Then I who came out first will stand there as an anchor for all to come through by performing the same deed. You will be drawn by a fiery brooding upon this wonderful mystery, drawn to the Risen Christ, who is formed out of all. As you enter we fuse, and the mortal you, reassumes immortality. You fell into the mortal state in order to experience death, and when you turn around, you rise to become one with immortality.

I tell you: you are the Lord God Jehovah, who conceived the play and deliberately entered it. You did nothing wrong. It was an adventure and without adventure, what is life? If someone left you a billion dollars so you could be cushioned for the rest of your life here, they would be robbing you of your creative adventure. In the beginning you left all by emptying yourself of all that you were aware of being. Then you took upon yourself the form of a slave. Wearing a slave–mask right now, no one knows who you really are, and you cannot recognize those who you have known throughout all eternity.

Bennie came to my home a week ago, and sitting beside him I could see nothing but love pouring forth from him. I couldn't see his face, for his skin is dark, but when I looked at Bennie all I could see was the being of love I knew in eternity. In the beginning we were all the Elohim, which is a compound unity of one made up of others. Bennie has as dark a skin as I have ever seen on a man, and I am as fair as man can be, so you might think we came out of different beings – but these are only masks we wear. Bennie has turned around and now knows he is the light of the world. He knows he is infinite love.

May I tell you: when you see infinite love, you will see Man. You will see he who is the gathering togetherness of all! I will know you by the light and you will know me by the light; but when we know each other as One, it will be as Love, and that is Man. Everyone is gathered into the human form divine! Not one will be lost, for in the beginning we agreed to dream this world into being, in concert. Then we went our separate ways, to falling into different states of consciousness and blaming others for the discords in our world. That's all right, for one day we will return and all the discords will be resolved into perfect harmony, as we expand beyond what we were prior to the play.

You can put me to the test tonight by learning how to move. My brother Victor learned how to move into riches when he had nothing. Living on borrowed money and trying to operate a little shop on a side street, Victor would stand before one of the largest buildings in the island and see "J.N. Goddard and Sons" on the marquee, rather than the existing "F.N. Roach and Company". This he did every day until the idea was fixed in his mind's eye. Two years later, the business failed. (You may think that was wrong, but nothing is wrong in God's name. We ate of the tree of millennium and fell into right and wrong). When the building was put up for sale, a man we hardly knew bought it for my brother, and the sign was changed from "F.N. Roach and Company" to "J.N. Goddard and Sons".

What did my brother do? He moved his imagination. He had no money when he purchased the building in 1922. Now, in 1967, I don't think you could buy the family out for $25 million. I own ten per cent of the stock, but I do not know its value. I came here to tell you, not how to make money, but how to operate the law of identical harvest so that if everything is taken from you tonight you can rebuild it tomorrow.

This is how it works. I imagined myself into what I am, and I can imagine myself into what I want to be. I am forever becoming what I imagine myself to be, be it good, bad, or indifferent. There is no deity on the outside who condemns and causes you to do what you are doing. You moved into the state you are now occupying either wittingly or unwittingly, for God and your own wonderful human Imagination are one. So, when you say: "I and my Father are one" you are speaking of your human imagination!

I have been sent to clarify scripture and take off the barnacles off the story called Jesus Christ. This is a small beginning, but what does it matter? You who hear me will tell the story and bring it back to somewhere near its original form, for the story as interpreted by the churches of the world is not anything near the truth. This morning I read Buckley's column. I enjoy his use of words and I find him quite an interesting fellow. Today he wrote about the Bishop of Canterbury, saying: "I don't believe the good Bishop would recognize a Christian if he met one, or scripture if he read it." I don't always agree with Buckley, but this time I agreed, after reading what he quoted the Bishop as having said. Now, this is not only true of the present bishop but of all the bishops I have met, whether they call themselves cardinals or popes, for their rituals, beliefs, and teachings are so far removed from the true story of Jesus.

I am here to tell you that God became you! How? By seeing the mask (one like you see in Africa or in Hawaii) and identifying himself with it. Now disguised as that which God wears, you can no longer see who you really are. But I tell you: the being behind the mask you now see as your brother, your sister, your wife, your husband and children – is a part of the Elohim who created the play and is playing every part. One day that being will take off the mask and you will resurrect and leave your empty skull. So, I say to my friend who saw the mask with the empty skull made of plastic: the day will come when you will ascend with one of us whose mask is already taken off, and pointing to that skull, you will say of it: "I once dwelt there." Then you will know as I do that you were never the mask you wore. And in eternity we will all know each other and all be enhanced beyond what we were, by reason of the journey that we made.

Tonight, you try this. Test it. Learn how to move. The test is simple. Just like my brother, take a simple little thing like asking yourself: "What do I want?" Now, looking at the world as you now see it, if you had what you wanted, would you continue to see the world as it is now? I doubt it. It need not be a change from where you live, but if there were a change you would see the world differently and, naturally your closest circle of friends would see a changed you. Well, begin to move in God by seeing your world from a different angle, and let your friends see you there. You are the operant power and move in your own being.

If you move from where you are to where you would like to be, you could detect that motion only by a change of position relative to another object. Motion in itself cannot be done without some frame of reference from which it moves. If your income had just been increased to say $30,000 a year from your present income of less than $10,000, how would you feel? How would your present circle of friends see you? Would they know it? Would they discuss it? Would they speak of the change in your life? Tell them, and then eavesdrop and hear your friends discuss you as one who is now making $30,000 a year. That's a motion in God and that movement will produce results! Everything in this world is nothing more than the result of a movement in God, which is a motion in your wonderful imagination. The slightest imaginal act that is a change (I don't mean just an act, for you can imagine things you don't believe), but if you imagine something you believe is a change, a thrill is sent through divine being. At that moment you have actually entered another state and made it alive and real in your world!

Try it tonight. It costs you nothing, not even a nickel. But may I tell you that when you stand in the presence of the one being who is drawing all towards itself, you are sent into the world to tell them your fantastic story; and if they do not apply what you tell them, they become disillusioned and hate you who invited them to dream. I am sent to invite everyone to dream consciously, to dream deliberately, for this is a dream world. They say that where he comes, he is always rejected, for he tells man: "Whatever you desire, believe that you have received it and you will." Anyone who makes that bold assumption and gets the confidence of those whose sphere he reaches, runs the risk of rejection, for when they try it and do not quite know how to do it, they become disillusioned and invariably hate the one who invited them to dream. That's the risk every teacher who is sent must run.

But I tell you: it's true anyway, and if one fails to bring their dream into being and becomes embittered, I say to myself: "How often must I tell them? Seventy times seven." I must tell them until they really understand, and those who hear me, will carry my message forward. They will be heard and in the end, we will all be gathered back into the one being, to know that we were that one being who conceived the play and took the plunge. So, when we said in the beginning: "It is time for the play to begin," not one of us failed to respond in the first person, present tense: "I AM".

Now let us go into the silence.

A Parabolic Revelation

It is in you as a person that the nature of God is revealed, for a scriptural episode is not a record of an historical event, but a parabolic revelation of truth. To see Jesus or David as an historical character is to see truth tempered to the weakness of your soul. You must see what the characters represent, rather than the characters themselves. This is true for every story in scripture, for every episode will unfold within you.

The title of the 54th Psalm is translated as "David is hiding with us" in the King James Version, and "David is in hiding among us" in the Revised Standard Version; but the title should read: "David is in hiding within us," for that is where he is, as well as every character in scripture. When I say, with Blake: "All that you behold, though it appears without it is within, in your Imagination of which this world of mortality is but a shadow," I mean that literally, for the drama of life unfolds from within.

The characters Jesus, David, Abraham, and Moses are but personifications of eternal states, which you individually will encounter as you move towards the ultimate awakening of being God himself. In his poem, "Saul" Robert Browning tells the story recorded in the 16th chapter of the Book of First Samuel, of how David cured Saul of the evil spirits which the Lord had sent upon him.

Do not see Saul as a man, but as humanity. He is the human being referred to in the 4th chapter of the Book of Daniel: "And the great watcher said 'Hew down the tree, cut off its branches, scatter its leaves and its fruit, but leave the stump.'" Then the tree becomes personified as: "Let him be watered with the dew from heaven; and let him move with the beasts of the earth. Take from him the mind of man and give him the mind of a beast. Let seven times pass over him until he knows that the Most High rules the kingdom of men and gives it to whom he will, even the lowliest of men." Saul personifies the mind of the beast, for Saul went insane; he was violent and could not remember who he was. Then David appears and cures him of his insanity by telling him of the coming of the Messiah, saying:

> *"O Saul, it shall be*
> *A Face like my face that receives thee; a Man like to me,*
> *Thou shalt love and be loved by, forever: a Hand like this hand*
> *Shall throw open the gates of a new life to thee! See the Christ*
> *stand!"*

You may think this is an episode in the pages of history, but it is a drama, which will take place in you. As an insane being who is looking for an external savior, one day you will encounter David – he who never walked the face of the earth – and save yourself!

All revelations have the mode of certainty about them. When David stands before you, you who were insane only a moment before, having forgotten who you are, will remember. Then, as Saul, you will see the true relationship between you and your son, and the revelation as to who you really are. Then you who were formerly Saul will become Paul, and say: "Henceforth I regard no one from the human point of view, even though I once regarded Christ from the human point of view, I regard him thus no longer."

Paul was trained to believe in an external, historical past of Israel. To him David was the king of kings. But when God revealed his son *in* him, Paul claimed he did not see anyone as flesh and blood. What man, believing in the historicity of scripture, could understand what Paul was talking about, when he was the one who formerly tormented anyone who would not accept the historicity of the Old Testament! But, when discussing the Messiah, Paul confessed that he could no longer believe in any historical character of the Old Testament. (The New, of course had not been written yet). Through revelation Paul knew who the Messiah was and who the Lord was. Seeing himself as the Lord, the one the world believes to be Jesus, Paul knew that what the world believed to be a mighty king was his only begotten son who was never flesh and blood. He knew the entire episode took place in the spirit, and said: "When it pleased God to reveal his son in me, I discussed it not with flesh and blood."

To see Jesus, Abraham, Moses, Jacob, or any of the characters of scripture as men of flesh and blood and external to yourself in the pages of history, is to see truth tempered to the weakness of your soul, because until the revelation takes place, you are unable to stand the force of the light of revelation. There is nothing more difficult than to give up a fixed idea, especially concerning religion or politics. Born into a certain religious group, your mother taught you what she was taught by her mother. The school and church you attend confirms your mother's words and you believe that the characters of scripture lived in time and space and left behind a record of their physical existence – when it isn't so at all. These are all revelations of an eternal drama which is in you, for your true being is your own wonderful human imagination.

Many times, I have been asked if I believe there was once a man called Jesus, and I always answer, "No." I did believe it, but I no longer believe in the historicity of any character of scripture, for I encounter them as personified states. I have entered the final state, which is Jesus, and in that state it was revealed to me that I am Jesus and Christ is my son. Christ, my creative power and wisdom, is the one who was anointed with the oil of gladness and called David. It was in the spirit that David called Jesus, Father. He does not do this in flesh for, if you take the events chronologically you will see that they are separated in time by one thousand years – and I tell you the story is contemporary. It is not something of the past. The Lord Jesus is with you now at this very moment, for he is your very being, your reality. We are told that he is a Father in the 17th chapter of John, as: "Holy Father, keep them in thy name that thou hast given me, that they may be one even as we are one." The Father/son is an inner action relationship. At one moment the son is speaking, and the next moment it is the Father who speaks; then without warning he jumps back to that of the son, and man is confused. Man thinks of one being of flesh and blood when it is an inner–relationship of Father/son.

I received a letter this week from a lady who is here tonight. In a vision she saw a man and his young son sitting at a table. At that moment she knew she was the son and the father and that they were one. Now, this same lady had another vision in which a friend proclaimed to the crowd in a very loud voice that the lady was pregnant and was bringing forth the Son of God. She is right, for this lady is bringing forth the Son of God, as she *is* God. This son will be born not of blood, nor of the will of the flesh, nor of the will of man, but of

God. She is the Jesus of scripture, bringing forth God, and because God is a Father his last gift to her is himself.

If God is the Father and he gives you himself, he gives you his son to reveal it. So, he sends the Spirit of his son into your heart, crying: "Father." And if God's son calls you Father, then you must be God. And if God the Father is the Lord Jesus and Christ is his anointed one, then your son is David, for he is the one the Lord anointed, and proclaimed: "Thou art my son, today I have begotten thee." This comes as a great shock to those who were raised in the Christian or Jewish faith, for there is no more historicity in the characters of the Old Testament then there is in the New. Every character represents an eternal state through which you, an individual, must pass in your journey from darkness to light. And when you come to the journey's end you move into the state personified as God the Father.

David is in hiding within us. This we are told by the Ziphites, of the tribe of Judah. If you read scripture correctly you will see that the only son of Jacob mentioned in the genealogy of Jesus is Judah. This brings us to Saul, who was notified that David was hiding within him. As an insane man, Saul could not understand. If David is hiding within me, where do I look for him? But wait. David will come out. I know. At one moment in time there will be an explosion within you which will release David, who is hiding in you, for we are all the insane of Daniel. Look at the world today and ask yourself if we aren't all insane, when we murder each other and cheat one another – when there really is no other. The prayer is that they be one as we are one. That is because they do not realize we are all one being. Nothing can bring you to this realization other than the revelation of the son to the Father.

I know so many of you are bringing forth the Son of God. Another lady in this audience tonight wrote saying she was sleeping at the home of a friend, when she sees a baby boy, devoid of clothes, lying on a blanket. As she picks it up she hears the doorbell ring. Answering the door with the child in her arms, she sees her daughter, who says: "Mother, put some clothes on your baby because I have brought a friend." As they enter the house the friend pats the baby on the back and says: "What a beautiful child." She returns to the room and as she covers the baby with a blanket (the swaddling cloth) she awakens. This is a wonderful adumbration forecasting the real event recorded in scripture. Then she will know the truth concerning the birth of God.

Another lady saw the child as her sister's boy. Holding it close she looked into its face, which turned into that of a cherub, who smiled at her. Then she knew she could not give the child up as it was hers. This, too, is an adumbration. All of these are foreshadowing. These ladies are all mothers with children of their own. The last lady has five children; yet the child of their vision is spiritual, for the whole Bible from beginning to end is a supernatural document and not an historical fact as man has been led to believe.

If you see Jesus as an historical character, it is because you do not have the courage to face the brilliant light of the revelation of truth. I know when it came to me, everything within me fell. We are told that in the end all of the buildings will fall. These buildings are the structures of the mind by which we live. The belief in the historicity of Jesus is a building; the belief in the historicity of the Bible is a building. Externalized as churches and cathedrals, they are beautiful, but they will all fall within you in your last days. And from their ashes that which is permanent will rise, for from then on you will not live by any external belief. You will know that everything unfolds from within.

The story is told that Judas would go into a garden and give a sign designating the one who holds the secret. The sign was a kiss. You will find this story in the 14th chapter of the Book of Mark. When you read it you may think this is an episode which took place in some historical past, but it is not. It is something you will experience. Then you will discover that the drama is contemporaneous. It is with us now, for I have had that experience.

I am teaching the word of God from experience, therefore, I am the word that went out. I sent it out from myself by clothing myself in flesh (for the Word became flesh and dwells within). When all that the Word implies unfolded in me I told my experiences to a group of twelve men, and when one departed I knew he was going to reveal my teaching. Then a handsome, wonderful man entered to fulfill the 14th chapter of Mark: "This is the sign I give you. The one I shall kiss is the man. Treat him kindly, but do not let him go." (If this is the truth don't let go, for it is the truth that I am going to kiss.) Approaching me, the man extends his arms in adoration, embraces me, and kisses me on the left side of my neck.

Now, the word "Judah" means, "to praise with extended arms." It was Judah who embraced and kissed me, he severed my sleeve revealing the arm of the Lord, thus fulfilling scripture. "And who has believed our report? To whom has the arm of the Lord been revealed?" The arm is the symbol of the creative power of God. That is what was revealed in its beautiful imagery. Here was a handsome man, about forty, gloriously dressed, fulfilling everything scripture said he would do when he comes. Believe my words, for they are true. Let everything you formerly believed in go – but do not let the word of truth go.

I know it is difficult to give up the belief in the historicity of scripture. When I first came to Los Angeles it was back in 1945. At the time I was invited by a very prominent man in the metaphysical field to conduct a series of lectures on the Bible. The night I arrived, I was to address 400 or 500 of his graduates. About five minutes before I took the platform, the man took me aside and told me that I could not speak on the non–historicity of the Bible, because he teaches the Bible as history and did not want his people disturbed. I thanked him, told him that because I was his guest I would abide by his decision this night, but in the future, he could not tell me what to say. Then I reminded him of scripture: "Whether it is right in the sight of God to listen to you rather than to God, you must judge." I can only speak of what I have seen and heard. I know the Bible is not historically true, but is eternally true. The records recorded there are forever and to be experienced by all.

Scripture is a revelation of truth which carries with it such certainty it cannot be denied. Having heard the truth from someone who has experienced it, you may feel my message is too much to grasp; but when it happens in you doubt leaves, for you know the truth from experience. Every story is true, but not as recorded. They were not writing secular history, but divine or sacred history, which is forever. It is not something that happened in the past or that will come; the climax has been reached and is always being reached every moment in time.

The Jesus of scripture is seated here tonight. And his son, bearing witness to his Fatherhood, is hiding in you. In the 54th Psalm, Saul was told that David was hiding within, just as I am telling you now. David is hiding in you and will come out when an explosion takes place within you. And when you see David he will be standing. That is why I believe Browning had the experience, because the symbolism he used is perfect. "See the Christ stand!" When I saw David, I was seated but he was standing.

The word "Christ" means the "the messiah." Standing before Saul, David tells of the coming of the messiah, saying: "His face will be like my face. He will be a man like me. You are going to love the messiah and he will love you forever." This relationship between you and David is one of infinite love and it is forever. Here David is telling Saul that he is the messiah, for he is the Christ, the anointed of the Lord. Then he said: "A hand just like this hand will open the door of a new life to you." And standing before him, he says: "See the Christ stand" – but Saul could not understand.

Those who read Browning miss this point because it is in conflict with their fixed ideas concerning Jesus. They think he is the Christ, but I tell you: Jesus is God the Father whose final revelation to man is the gift of himself. God gives himself to you by sending his son into your heart, crying: "Father," thus revealing your true identity. Until then you do not know that you are Jesus and remain confused by the hearing of many different beliefs.

I speak of this only from the platform where you come to hear it, but I would never go into your home and volunteer this information. That would be silly and completely out of order. I would be taking my pearls and throwing them before those who are not yet qualified to receive them, so I do not disturb them. But you who know it are called upon to voice what you know. And you who are moved to teach – teach the true words of the pattern which I have given you, but do change the pattern. Paul called the pattern "my gospel." Paul was very proud of the fact that he was born a Jew, saying: "I was born of the seed of Abraham, of the tribe of Benjamin, a Pharisee of the Pharisees." Then the whole thing unfolded within him and he realized the non–historicity of his own great Book, yet its truth. He recognized the characters recorded there as eternal state through which every individual must pass.

One day you will experience the state of Abraham and know what faith really is. When you see that giant of a man leaning against a tree, you will see a serpent wound around its trunk. The serpent will have a human face with the wisest expression. (In Genesis the serpent is recorded as the wisest of all of God's creatures.) And you will see Abraham's eyes are looking into time, as recorded in the Book of Galatians: "The scripture, foreseeing that God would justify all by faith, preached the gospel beforehand to Abraham." So, before the events took place Abraham was shown the end, and when you look at him his attention is focused, not on the distance of space, but of time. And the tree under which he stands looks like the human brain. When you see Abraham, you will know you are seeing the beginning of the journey. Wisdom is present in the form of a serpent and faith is present in the form of Abraham. His name is changed from Abram – which means "exalted Father" to Abraham – which means "father of the multitude." The change occurred when the letter "*He*" was added. This letter carries the symbol of grace. So, grace was put into the name to indicate that God had given himself to his creation (the work of his hand.) Putting the gift of grace into the name of the father of the multitudes, the journey begins.

So, when you read scripture try to bear in mind that you are reading about infinite states of consciousness, which are eternal. Remember, you are Jesus, and when you find the Christ you have found the Lord's anointed, who is David. You will know him for he will come to you in the spirit and call you Father. How then can you be his son? Because the words Father/son are interchangeable. "I and my Father are one. He who sees me (the son) sees the Father." Always keep this in mind when reading scripture.

If you will accept what I have told you this night, life will be much easier for you. Knowing this truth, you can't pass the buck anymore; but knowing you are the Lord you can do anything, because you are all imagination and imagining creates reality. You can imagine anything and sustain it with faith. As you walk in the faith that that which you have imagined is so, it will become so. This I know from experience.

Back in 1943 when I came out of the army I was looking for an apartment. My wife and I had determined how much we were going to pay for it, but when we found the apartment the rent was more than we had planned to pay. Realizing this, my wife said: "Well, that's not demonstrating this principle, is it." I said nothing. I simply paid the months of September and October, but when I went to pay the November rent the manager said: "I have an apology to make to you. An authority of the city came in and looked over my books. He discovered that the apartment you have was formerly rented for less." Then he quoted the new rent figure to me, which was to the dollar the amount I had originally chosen to pay. It took me three months of being faithful to what I had imagined I was paying, even though during that time I was paying more. But, since the reduced rent was retroactive to the day I moved in, I got it all back at the beginning of the third month.

I committed myself in my imagination, to what I was going to pay. I went looking, and because I was going to pay more – in his eyes – he gave me all kinds of concessions he would not have done had I paid him what the former tenant did. First of all, he allowed us to pick out the wallpaper, the colors and rooms we wanted painted. He even built a bookshelf for me which covered an entire wall, for all my books. He did everything I wanted; but if I had gone in there and gotten the rent for the amount I said I would pay, he would not have built the bookcase for me, given me the wallpaper, or painted the entire apartment to my specifications. Only then was the rent reduced to the amount I had imagined it to be, and we remained there almost fourteen years.

I tell you: imagination will not fail you if you are faithful. What could I say when I was confronted with the negation of my assumption? Nothing. I simply would not give up, and when the time was right my assumption became a fact. I urge you to set your goal high. Assume the feeling it has been reached and sleep in that feeling. Persist and I promise you that not one thing in this world can rob you of that which you have assumed. But the most important thing is to know that which is housed within you is God's plan of redemption, and he only redeems himself. God came down into the world and housed himself in you. Now he is going to discover who he is, for it is in you as a person that the nature of God is revealed.

Now let us go into the silence.

A Prophecy

In his poem called "Europe," which is a prophecy about you, William Blake said: "Then Enitharmon woke, nor knew that she had slept, and eighteen hundred years were fled as if they had not been."

Told in the form of a story, Blake used the name "Enitharmon" to express any emanating desire or image. Enitharmon is the emanation of Los, who – in the story – had the similitude of the Lord and all imagination. Entering into his image (his Enitharmon), Los dreams it into reality; and when he awoke he knew not that he had slept, yet eighteen hundred years had fled.

In my case, 1,959 years had fled as though they had not been. And I had no idea I had entered into an image called Neville and made it real. But I, all imagination, so loved the shadow I had cast, I entered into it and made it alive.

To those in immortality I seemed to be as one sleeping on a couch of gold, but to myself I was a wanderer. Although lost in dreary night, I kept the divine vision in time of trouble. I kept on dreaming I was Neville until I awoke, not knowing I had slept; yet 1,959 years had fled as though they had not been.

Blake tells us that in the beginning we were all united with God in a death like his. Then we heard the story and entered into our shadows. Now, a shadow is a representation, either in painting or drama, in distinction from the reality portrayed. Paul recognized the shadow when he asked the Galatians: "Who has bewitched you, before whose eyes Jesus Christ was publicly portrayed as crucified. Let me ask you only this: did you receive the spirit by works of the law or by hearing with faith? Are you so foolish, having begun with the spirit are you now ending with the flesh, by seeing Jesus Christ as someone on the outside?"

Having heard the story of Jesus Christ, you are called upon to enter into it as the central character and remain there until the story externalizes itself.

God destined us, in love, to be his sons through Jesus Christ according to the purpose of his will. Falling in love with his image, God entered it and became his son. Having declared what he was going to do, God does it through his pattern called Jesus Christ.

Knowing what you want, when you conceive a scene that implies you have it, that objective becomes the pattern for your desire to unfold. Jesus Christ is God's pattern, his purpose which he set forth for the fullness of time. Christ is the plan, the image God entered and made so real he claims he is the image.

God's plan has completely unfolded in me. When I awoke I knew not that I had slept, and 1,959 years were fled as though they had not been. This is true for every child born of woman, for we were all gathered together and united with him in a death like his; therefore, we shall certainly be united with him in a resurrection like his.

Blake, writing in 1794, knew that 1,800 years had fled when he – Enitharmon – awoke. Blake knew he was the emanation, the shadow God entered and identified himself with. Blake tells us it was the image that awoke, knowing not that she had slept.

The emanation is always feminine. Eve came out of Adam. Every desire is feminine, regardless of what it is, be it a house, money, or a new car. Imagination is the male, which must leave every doubt, every thought of impossibility behind, and cleave to the desired emanation until they are one. To do this, imagination must enter into the shadow and remain there until there is only the awareness of being or possessing the fulfilled desire.

In this world of Caesar, it could take an hour, a day, a week, or a month, to awaken the desire within and project it on the screen of space. But you must enter into the image and remain there, just as God did in the foundation of time, in order to make you, himself. God so became me, that when He awoke in the tomb, I did not know I had slept. In fact, I did not know I had been placed there, as I had become so one with it.

In his book of Milton, Blake tells us that when he entered into his shadow, he appeared to those in immortality as one asleep on a couch of gold. But to himself he was a wanderer, lost in dreary night. Is that not the story of everyone? Lost and confused, imagination is faithful to the image he has assumed, saying: I am John, I am Ray, or I am Natalie.

Now in the image of the being I fell in love with, Neville is my emanation, my shadow, and the image I have been faithful to. Many a time I have thought myself a wanderer in dreary night, confused and not knowing where to turn for a dollar. But those who contemplate on death saw me as one asleep on a couch of gold. They knew the purpose behind my entering into the state of sleep, but they did not know what I was experiencing.

You are in this world because you are in love with the being you believe yourself to be. You may say that is not true, but I say it is impossible for thought greater than itself to know. Do not believe anyone who claims to know. Do not believe anyone who claims to love someone else more than they do themselves, for they do not. It is impossible for thought to be greater than the image it believes itself to be. Yes, you want companionship, security, and health, for these are all part of the image you fell in love with and entered.

You are now alive because you – a living being – have given the image called by your earthly name, life. And you will transform it into a life–giving spirit, because that is what you really are. Before this drama called life began, you predetermined a perfect pattern called Jesus Christ, which would lead you back to where you were prior to entering into the image.

Now, in this world a man who wants to be a success in business can sit down and map out a pattern (a scene) which would imply he has the success he desires. Then if he enters the scene and believes its truth, the pattern of success will unfold and the world will confirm it. But he must persist in the image of success, just as God has persisted, for the day will come when God will awaken and express the success he believes himself to be.

God enters into the image of every child born of woman to give it life. At that moment God's real and immortal self is – to those who dwell in immortality – as one sleeping on a couch of gold; but to himself he seems a wanderer, lost in dreary night. The day will come when he will awake and – unknown to him, 1800 or 2000 years will have fled as if they had not been.

Use the same technique God used to become you. As one whose name forever is I AM, God fell in love with you, his image, and entered it. Now knowing you are, you say I am; so,

God is occupying his image and now answers to the name you were given at birth.

Intrigued by the idea of expressing himself in a body of flesh and blood, God entered this body by dreaming he is Neville. God laid himself down within me to sleep, and as he slept he dreamed he was I; for 1,959 years later, when God awoke, I knew not that I had slept. And, upon reflection, it was as though it had not been; for when God achieved his objective (which was to awake) and was conscious of the fact that he was the one he loved, all time vanished.

Before awakening there are barriers that separate God and his image, but once his objective is achieved, God awakes to the awareness that He and his image are one. This is the story the world celebrates and calls Christmas.

Christmas is not the incarnation of God, but the awakening of man as God. Having fallen asleep and entering his image, God made it a living being. In Blake's case it took 1800 years. Why does it take one 2,000 and another 1,000 years to awaken? It depends upon the degree God is lost in the dream.

To what degree are you lost in your dream of success? Your world is your dream pushed out. When you can persuade yourself 100% that you are successful, success is yours! You must become so intense that you completely forget it was only a desire. You must tame the wild, new state you have entered until its naturalness causes you to forget all else. That is how God became you.

Jesus Christ, God's pattern of salvation begins to unfold as you awake and resurrect from the tomb God entered. Being life itself, God entered you – his shadow, which has no life of its own – and made it alive. Entering death's door, his image –

God – lay down in the grave of that image, in visions of eternity until he awakes.

In the Old Testament, the question is asked: "Rouse thyself, O Lord, awake. Why cast us off forever?" And in the New Testament, the Lord awakens to discover he is one with the image he fell in love with. Having fallen in love with being you, individually, when God awakes, you are He. That is Christmas.

When God incarnated himself in the image he so fell in love with, time was divided between BC and AD. Blake tells us that for him, it took 1800 years for God to move from BC to AD. In my case it was 1,959 years. Each case is different, as we are told: "Each in his own order." I do not know whether this order was predetermined or not, for the Book of Ephesians tells us that he destined us in love to be his sons through Jesus Christ according to the purpose of his will.

The God that dreamed in me is the same God that dreams in you. Was it really an order that I could not have awakened before 1959? I do not know. I only know that was the year in which God awoke in me, yet I did not know I had fallen asleep in that skull. But when I emerged, the symbolism recorded as revealing the birth of God surrounded me. That was the moment God awoke and was born into a higher region of his being. Having identified himself with the one he loved, that one was raised and born as God.

God is in love with his image, his shadow, which – like a reflection on oil or water – is dead. Having no life in itself, God so loves his shadow he enters it and dreams he is it. Being a life–giving spirit, God first animates the shadow and it becomes solid and real in his world. He walks and talks, knows sorrow and joy, sickness and health, until the dream is complete. Then God awakens a pattern by which he will know he has arrived at the end.

This pattern was predetermined. The first segment is to awaken and rise from his sleep of death, to be designated Son of God in power. Then he discovers his fatherhood when his son calls him father. A short interval later he cuts himself in two. This is his sacrifice for this wonderful accomplishment. Fusing with his blood, which he finds at the base of his spine, God ascends as a fiery serpent. Then the final sanctification comes in the form of a dove, which descends and smothers him with love, for God has now accomplished what he set out to do.

You can imitate God while here in this world. If, for example you desire to be a great artist, acclaimed throughout the country, map out a plan of success, just as God mapped out a plan of fulfillment which he called Jesus Christ. There are multiple ways to imagine success. Choose a scene which would imply you already have achieved success and when it unfolds, you will know how it came about. Do this, and you are testing the infinite power that you really are.

Having entered the shadow that I conceive myself to be, I walk the earth wondering where the next dollar is coming from; yet those in great eternity see me as dreaming on a golden couch. But I am still faithful and keep the divine vision in time of trouble. Then, like a woman in labor who bears its pains, after the child is born the pain is forgotten in the job of fulfillment, so it is when Christmas comes and you – individualized – become God.

The same technique God used to make you real can be used to bring your desire into being. Blake said: "If the spectator could only enter into the image in his imagination, approaching it on the fiery chariot of contemplative thought;

if he could only make a friend and companion of one of these images, he would rise from the grave and meet his Lord in the air and then he would be happy."

God entered into his image, therein giving us life. Being a life–giving spirit, God wants us to be just as he is, so he mapped out the pattern that through it we may be God. When we completely fulfill his predetermined pattern, the barrier will be torn down and we will be one with infinity.

Christmas as celebrated by the Christian world is not Christmas. It is not something that takes place on the outside. Christmas consists of a series of events which begin when God awakens within the shadow He entered. Rising, God desires to come out; and since all things are possible to God, He pushes, and a seemingly unbreakable seal falls away and infinite power comes out.

The predetermined symbolism must be there. If it isn't, then the vision is an adumbration indicating nearness. It is a shadow cast before coinciding with the actual vision.

These visions are recorded in the four gospels, of which three were written in or about 150 AD. Scholars believe the Book of John was written at the end of the first century, however, making it possible for him to draw on the source material of all the others.

John eliminates the story of a genealogy, or virgin birth, but emphasizes the need of rebirth. He doesn't tell you how it is done, but using the word *anothin*, meaning the birth is from above.

There are two births: The first is from the womb of woman and the second from the tomb above, and each birth is essential. Also, you must rise in the same manner as Moses raised the serpent in the desert.

John claims that God Himself became you, saying: "In the beginning was the Word, and the Word was with God, and the Word was God. The Word became flesh and dwells in us." Here we see that God became flesh – as you are – and says, "I am". So, God is incarnated as an animated being, but that is not enough. He wants you to be as He is, and God is a life–giving spirit. In order to do this his pattern must be fulfilled. And when it is, you enter an entirely different sphere, called the kingdom of heaven.

Having fallen in love with your image, God entered that shadow and made it alive by falling asleep. Now dreaming he is human, he loves you – the being you identify with today. You may not be in love with being poor, but that is not you! You could be rich if that is your desire, but you are in love with being yourself! You would not give up your individuality for any other being. You may desire to have what someone else has, but not if you have to give up your identity.

At one time, that which you have so identified yourself with was only a shadow, an image God entered. It was dead, and by God's entry, He made it a living being. And when God awakes, that living being becomes a life–giving spirit.

If it is a true awakening, and not just a foreshadowing, the drama called Jesus Christ will unfold in 1,260 days, as foretold in scripture. Do not be discouraged if your visions are foreshadowings; the promise will be fulfilled, for you are keeping the vision in time of trouble. At times, like Peter you may have denied that you are God, but you are still keeping the divine vision.

I fell in love with being Neville, as you fell in love with the being you are now. You have dreamed poverty into being, health, being loved, being ignored, but you have never lost your vision of individuality You will never lose it, for that is the one you fell in love with. And in the end, you will awaken as God, individualized. You will know yourself to be a life–giving spirit as you move towards ever greater and greater individualization. That is the purpose of the entire drama, and that is what Christmas means.

When it will happen, I do not know. Blake certainly was not 1800 years old judged by the world of Caesar. He was born in 1757 and wrote his poem, "Europe" in 1794. Blake was speaking of that second birth, believing that if we have been united with Christ in a death like his, we shall be united with him in a resurrection like his. Blake looked upon this division of time between BC and AD as the beginning, claiming he was one with God when, falling in love with his image, he became universally diffused individuality. Starting as we did, the God in him took 1800 years to complete the drama and awaken.

In his poem, "Europe," Blake speaks of the cavern man and his five openings. His eyes, which see only a small section of infinity. His ears, which will hear the music of the heavens. His breath and mouth, totaling four; but Blake does not tell us where the fifth one is. He does, however, tell us that through this opening man may leave at any time and return, but man does not choose to do so. What is that one but imagination? Standing here, I can imagine myself elsewhere. What opening do I use to imagine myself there? The fifth one of the five openings of the cavern man.

Soon the Christian world will celebrate this wonderful mystery, which is completely misunderstood. But one day you, individuality, will experience scripture and know the true mystery of Christmas. Then you, too, will say I woke and knew not that I had slept.

The sensation is one of waking, not resurrection. You know you are in your tomb, yet your skull. Because of an innate knowledge, you will push from within, and the stone will roll away as you are born from above.

Three witnesses will be there; two will deny your birth, and one will confirm it, for you are fulfilling scripture: "Where two or more persons agree in testimony, it is conclusive." One witness declares you as the father of the sign, the child wrapped in swaddling clothes. You – the father – witness the event, and scripture – the written word of God – bears you out; so you have three witnesses, all agreeing in testimony: the Bible, you, and a third.

This is the story of Christmas, the time when the prophecy made to you before that the world was, is fulfilled.

Now let us go into the silence.

A Riddle

Tonight I will call this, "A Riddle," for every creative mind rises to the challenge of a riddle. Now a riddle is defined in the dictionary as "an imperial object or person; that which is difficult to understand." It is also "a sieve to separate the chaff from the wheat, or a puzzling question."

Now I ask you: who is the greatest of the great of earth, who was never mortal born, or lived — as you and I understand the term — in this secular world? I could use the plural and say "they" who were never mortal born, but tonight I will confine myself to the greatest of the great of earth, the one that is worshiped by all. As far as I am concerned, he is Jesus Christ.

I think you will agree with me when I say you did not choose the environment in which you first found yourself at birth. But you quickly adjusted to everything you found here in this section of space/time; the habits, the classrooms, the religion, and the doctrine. This is true with everyone in the world. If they were honest with themselves, everyone would admit that they did not choose their environment, but simply found themselves there.

God the Father placed you in this particular age, as it is best suited for the work he is doing on himself in you. He did it willingly, prepared to accept all the consequences of this confused world of beings with all of its tangles and enigmas. This he did in Jesus Christ in you, for Christ is God's power and his wisdom buried in us all.

Now let us turn to scripture. We are told in the 6th chapter of Isaiah that the Lord God blinded their eyes and hardened their hearts, lest they turn and be saved. So, when someone awakens by reason of the long, long journey he has taken, and scripture fulfills itself in him and he tells it, there are only a few who will accept his message and believe him. The majority will reject him, for they will see only his mortal form in the world of men. They will know his father and mother, his sister and brothers. But when he tells them exactly how it unfolds and they cannot believe, so his story is completely discounted. But those who hear it and believe will experience scripture. They too will tell their experiences, yet it will still be denied by the mass because He has blinded their eyes and hardened their hearts, lest they see with their eyes and perceive with their hearts, turn and be saved.

Now, "Do you not believe that I am in the Father and the Father in me? That the words I speak are not my words, but the words of him who sent me? Believe that I am in the Father and the Father in me, for truly I say unto you, the work that I have done you shall do also and even greater works than these. If you don't believe me, believe it for the sake of the works themselves." God the Father is not on the outside. I am in the Father and the Father is in me. If you turn you will see Him and, becoming what you behold, you will vanish from sight. All that you see now, that appears so real before your face, is only a shadow made real by the world. This I know from experience.

There is a little boy in New York City who bears my name. He is now about fifteen. Before he was born he stood before me in vision and I felt I was his father. Appearing to be about four years old, he told me his name was Neville Mark. When I asked him when he was coming, he said the 10th of November. This was now September. The next morning, I told my wife that a little boy was coming to us on the 10th of November. Well, she admitted that she believed in miracles and in me, but she knew she was not pregnant. Regardless, I told her he was coming anyway.

A friend of mine who was expecting her baby in December wanted a little girl, as she already had a little boy. I said to her: "If your child is born on November 10th and it is a boy, his name is Neville Mark." She agreed, although she was certain that the child would be born in December. But when November 10th arrived, Neville Mark was born.

About five years ago, while visiting them in New York City, the little boy came in, walked over to me and said: "You know, Neville. I feel that if I could turn around I would see who I really am. I know I am wearing a mask and I can't wait to die, cause then I will turn around and see my true identity." His mother was a very poor girl who married wealth, and anything relative to death frightened her. The thought of losing her diamonds, her home, and all of her possessions, scared her to death, so she was upset when the child spoke of death. No doubt having grown up in the meantime, the boy's attention has been diverted; but that is what he told me five years ago.

Now let me tell you my own experience. While lying on the bed, on my left side, I felt a force coming from beyond my head – yet near it – enter it. The force as so powerful I wanted to turn around and see who was applying it. I felt as though some person – not an impersonal force but someone – was doing it. Although my body was just as alive as it is now, the force at the base of my skull was so intense I could not turn around. Had I turned, that day I would have seen the being that I am and instantly vanished from this world.

So, he blinded their eyes and hardened their hearts, lest they should see with their eyes and perceive with their hearts and turn and be saved. These same words are used, in the Greek sense, of the prodigal son who came to his senses and turned. Remembering his father, he turned and went home to receive the great robe, the ring, the fatted calf, and shoes for his feet.

You and I have been purposely blinded by the Father in us. Our hearts have been hardened by the Father in us. So, the words are true, and when you reach the end you will say: "Father forgive them for they know not what they do." God the Father uses the tyrants of the world for ends beyond their own. Every person in the world is only a mask God the Father wears while playing that part. Man sees and judges the mask; but the occupant he does not see, for his eyes have been blinded and his heart hardened. God is playing each part based upon the environment in which he was placed – not by his own choice, for we were made subject unto futility; – not willingly, but by the will of him who subjected us in hope; and we cannot turn back until His predetermined goal is reached. That is when we reach the end of the journey and go through the series of events called the story of Jesus Christ, at which time Christ is formed in you.

Christ is not and never was a mortal person. Those who believe that he was born from the womb of woman have no ears to hear and understand when told who Christ really is, or who the Father really is. To them "He who sees me sees the Father" is a riddle, which cannot be understood. But when the sum total of all experience of man is formed into a youth who calls you Father, the riddle is solved. David is he who sees you and thereby sees the Father; yet he, too, like the greatest of the great of earth, had no mortal birth.

Called Abraham, Isaac, Jacob, and Jesus Christ, you and I – clothed as we are in these mortal garments – make their drama alive; for it's the Father alone who is playing all the parts. Willing to take all the consequences of this horrible experience unto himself, in Christ, God the Father thinks Christ is other than the one who sent him; but he who sees me sees him who sent me: lo we are one.

The whole in me sent me to clothe myself in this garment of flesh you see. He placed me on the tiny island of Barbados in 1905, with many brothers, in a limited environment and no social, intellectual, or financial background. Then, because I was sifted prior to 1905 (the sifting was the riddle, separating the grains of wheat) I couldn't stand the environment I had been inducted into and felt the restlessness of a boy to continue my search. My one outstanding corporal punishment in this world was for the Bible. In response to my schoolmaster's question, I said, "Take up thy bed and walk." When he asked me for my Bible and I couldn't show it, he was allowed to beat me. I was beaten from my buttocks down to my feet for the Bible. But all of my life I have been restless for the Word of God. I came all the way across the ocean in my search and joined the theater, all in preparation to stand before you and tell you of my experiences.

I know from experience that if a man could only turn around, his eyes would no longer be blind or his heart hardened; for he would see that he and the very being who sent him into the world are one. You and your Father are one. You would see God's only begotten Son as a radiant being, the only God and you would see yourself as you really are.

Now, we are taught that all who are baptized into Christ have put on Christ, and all are one in Jesus Christ. This is true, for when you meet him, you are baptized. He who is infinite love sent you into this world of horror, where you murder and are murdered, rape and are raped, mutilate and are mutilated. And when you have experienced it all, you will turn and all is forgiven. Then you will return to your eternal home more brilliant because you have raised the one you wore.

"You must be perfect as your Father in heaven is perfect." The moment you turn, you are perfect, for you are the Father. Clothed in your body of perfection, the blind see, the deaf hear, the dumb shout for joy, as everything you behold is made perfect. I know, for it is the end of my journey. So, I say to you: be of good cheer. No matter what you have gone through, what you may still have to go through or what you are going through right now, one day you will be baptized into Jesus Christ, you will turn around and – seeing him – you are incorporated into his being.

To be baptized is to be completely covered with fluid. It doesn't mean water, because the Messiah is Christ and the Messiah is the placenta, one who is anointed with oil. What the pope does here hasn't a thing to do with it. There is a living fluid, living water you break through to merge with, just as a drop of water merges with the ocean; yet your identity or individuality is never lost.

All are One and all will be baptized into that One. All will put on the Lord, which simply means to live as, to move into the garment and flow with it. The last words of Christ in the Book of Luke are: "Remain in the city until you are imbued with power from on high." Power is Christ; wisdom is Christ, and to imbue is to clothe. In other words, wait until I have clothed you with myself, and on that day, you will literally say: "I am in Christ and Christ is in me."

Believe me when I tell you I am in the Father and the Father is in me. If you can't believe that, then believe it for the works themselves; for truly, truly I say unto you: the works that I do you shall do, and greater than these shall you do because I go unto the Father. I came out from the Father and came into the world. Again, I am leaving the world and returning to the Father.

The entire drama of scripture unfolds in us and hasn't a thing to do with any being that was mortal born. Christ in you who is your hope of glory is born from within, and does not walk the earth, as you who are born from the womb of woman. So, who is Christ? This, the riddle of riddles, is asked all through scripture. In the Book of Proverbs, the question is asked, "Who has established all of the ends of the earth? What is his name and what is his Son's name? Surely you know." Who has established all of the ends of the earth? The Father of fathers, one of infinite love, whose son is David. It is he who established all of the ends of the earth and sustains them from within you. You are his suffering servant, who is Himself.

The 53rd chapter of Isaiah, called "The Last of the Suffering Servants of God", begins: "Who has believed our report? And to whom has the arm of the Lord been revealed?" My arm has been revealed. It has been completely unveiled before those who are being prepared to tell the story.

So, I tell what has happened to me, but who will believe it? This power which is to be revealed in you is not worldly demonstration, but for the unfolding of your godhood. After your arm has been revealed, when you leave this world you are one at the right hand of the Father, for you are David, his right hand. God the Father unfolds himself in you, for there is nothing but God. Not God and you – just God.

You will discover diversity in unity as well as unity in diversity for, "Hear O Israel, the Lord our God is one Lord." Here is the compound unity, one made up of others. Diversity in unity as well as unity (I am) in death (diversity). I dwell in them and they dwell in me and we are one. Just as I am in the Father and the Father in me, I am (plural) and you (plural) are in me (singular). Here is diversity in unity. I look upon myself and see my world pushed out. Now I can see the diversity in unity as all within me. All that I behold, though it appears without, it is within me. All that I behold, though it appears without, it is within me in my own wonderful human imagination, of which this world of mortality is but a shadow.

May I tell you: it has been determined what the last will do, and how they will do it. Having become separated, all are moving toward the final event. I am not saying this to flatter you who attend my meetings, because whether you come or not, it makes no difference to my way of life. I am no longer interested in things of this world or to shine among shadows, for I know that the greatest of the great never walked the earth and was never mortal born. I have no desire to establish something here for shadows to say how wonderful I am. No, all of us are moving toward the inevitable end. To turn around as the prodigal son and be embraced by the Father, thereby becoming the Father. And on that day, you can forgive everyone, knowing they know not what they do. Believe me: every word of scripture is true, for I have experienced it. But it is not secular history. It is salvation history.

I heard Ben Gurion the other day on "Meet the Press." He is a grand old fellow of 80 now, who still sees the world as a history book and hasn't the slightest idea about scripture. Oh, he can quote it from cover to cover, but he's not alone. My sister's maid can quote the Bible from beginning to end, but she doesn't know a thing about life. Ben Gurion quotes the Bible beautifully, but he hasn't the slightest concept of who Abraham really is, or Isaac, or Moses, or Jacob, or any of these who were never mortal born. They are eternal spiritual states through which all men pass. Starting with the state of Abraham – the friend – the companion of the Father who is buried with him whispers in your ear and tells you the story of redemption. He tells you that you will be enslaved as long as you wear the garment of death. Then he will bring you up to have much, much more than you had before you entered; for God's power and his wisdom will be enhanced by reason of this challenge which God put upon himself. Then, in the end, you will turn around and see yourself as infinite love, fuse into and become one with the Everlasting Father. Everyone will turn to the Father and enter this wonderful unity of Christ. So here is diversity, and yet there is unity in diversity as there is diversity in unity.

You dwell upon what I have said tonight. It's a riddle, and riddles are difficult to understand. There is no greater riddle than this – the riddle of riddles, which is Christ. I tell you an incredible story. The story of one whose birth will influence all. Who tells the only truth. Who was born, yet was not mortal born. I tell you of one who dies, yet rose from the dead. This incredible story is summed up in one person, called Christ. He was not mortal born; he never walked the earth except within you; but rising from within, you experience everything that was said of Jesus in scripture, thereby un–riddling the riddle of Christ. The Old Testament is the riddle, and when Christ awakens within you, he un–riddles the riddle. Then when you tell of this un–riddled riddle, those who hear you will judge you by human standards, not knowing that the vision took place before you came into the world.

I was sifted a long time ago. I now know that I came into this world to be stirred in Christ. I was not satisfied with the environment into which I was placed at my mortal birth and became restless, knowing I was destined to grow into something different; so, I started my search to completely unveil the Christ in me, and now I am telling the story. I tell it to the best of my ability, but I know that only a few will hear it with faith. The mass will reject it. There will be those who will hear and believe, but they will be afraid of the reactions of society and, therefore will be silent. This is told us in the 12th chapter of John, where it is said that many heard and believed, "but for fear of the Pharisees they did not confess it lest they should be put out of the synagogue." The synagogue of the ancient world is still with us today, in all denominations of churches where anything that disagrees with their traditional concept of a secular is excommunicated.

Today the present pope is asking that Luther be brought back into the fold. He was excommunicated a hundred years ago and now they want to bring him back. Have you ever heard such nonsense? Isn't that "Alice in Wonderland"? How can you forgive a man who has been dead one hundred years? I tell you, forgive them for they know not what they do, and that goes for the pope down to the one who shines his shoes and thinks he's blessed because he is allowed to do it.

Let Christ awake in you and one day you will turn around and find joy in your return. I was sent into the presence of the Risen Christ. I didn't turn around. Had I turned around I would not be here. I was sent into his presence to answer the question asked of me, then to be incorporated into his body, that I may complete the journey. Any moment between now and my departure from this world I can turn around, and when I do, you will read of Neville's obituary. My journey is at its end. I have fought the good flight. I have finished the race. This I know from my own personal experience.

Tonight, I hope I have been able to un–riddle the riddle, for the greatest riddle in the world is in Jesus Christ, he who is your own wonderful human imagination.

Now let us go into the silence.

A State Called Moses

While reading scripture, always bear in mind that it is a story of salvation and not secular history, that the characters – from Adam to Jesus – are states of consciousness. In Blake's "Visions of the Last Judgment," he said: "It ought to be understood that the Persons Moses and Abraham are not here meant, but states signified by those names as they were revealed to mortal man in a series of divine revelations, as they are written in the Bible." Having seen the entire play, Blake added: "When you see them from afar they appear as one man, but as you approach they appear as multitudes of nations, as the One Man becomes the many."

The first five books of the Bible are called the Torah, or the Law, with Abraham as the symbol of the beginning of civilization. But the outstanding character recorded there is the infinite, eternal state called Moses. The word Moses is the old perfected (form) of the Egyptian verb "to be born"; so, it is in the state of Moses that something is to be born. Now, at the end of the Torah we are told: "Moses, the servant of the Lord died and the Lord buried him, but no man knows the place of his burial to this day." (*Deuteronomy 34*) Why? Because Moses is buried in you.

Today people try to perpetuate the identity of every prominent person in some mausoleum. In our country, daily trips are made to the graves of our presidents. I am told that there is not a day that Kennedy's grave is not covered with flowers, as people cry and pray there. So, we know the burial place of our presidents and heroes – but no one knows the burial place of Moses. Representing the future of Israel in germinal form, it is in Moses – a state buried in Man – that God's plan of redemption is revealed. Now, an Israelite is not a descendant of Abraham after the flesh, but the elect of God of any nation. Whether you be a Jew, Christian, or Mohammedan, Moses – the future of Israel in germinal form – is buried in you. And the word "Israel" means to rule as God.

Having seen the entire pattern of God's plan in the mountain, Moses returns and speaks to the people in the first person present tense, saying: "I am the Lord who brought you out of the land of Egypt, out of the house of bondage. You shall have no other gods besides me." Having said this, Moses reveals God's name as I am! He did not say, I am Moses and the Lord, but I am the Lord. Recognizing his true identity, Moses begins to do wonderful things, called signs. Giving Moses the rod of God, the Lord said: "Put upon it the fiery serpent, and everyone who sees it, whether he be ill or distressed, if he believes, he is healed." All of this beautiful imagery is literally true when God's plan begins to unfold in you.

We are told that Moses could not enter the promised land, that Joshua – filled with the spirit of wisdom – entered and the people followed. Joshua is the Hebraic word for Jesus. Moses could not enter because he is God's plan in germinal form. Joshua is its unfoldment, as the word says: "I am the Lord your God, the Holy One of Israel, your Savior and besides me there is no savior."

The plan unfolds in Joshua in the Old Testament, and Jesus in the New. If Joshua is filled with the wisdom of God, and Christ is defined as the power and wisdom of God, are they not one and the same being? God's glorious wisdom in germinal form saves Israel by pulling the one being out as the germ erupts. Then the man in whom it happens experiences the signs and wonders recorded in scripture in a literal manner. Who would have thought that the rod of God with a fiery serpent on it was literally true; yet I know it is the state you will experience as you enter the promised land.

I do not care how long you live or how much you own, you will die to this world. But you are destined to move into the land of the promise, a land that is eternal, where you cannot die. The garment of nature you now wear will die, but there is a germ in you called Moses that lives forever. He is buried in Golgotha, the skull of man. And the rod of God is your spinal cord. Having descended into division, God's creative power has gone down into generation. It is destined to be reversed and turned up into generation and unity.

There is only one creative being, only one God. Being protean, he appears to be unnumbered nations, races, and people; but in the end, one by one he gathers himself into the one body, the one Spirit, one Lord, one God and Father of us all –yet without loss of identity. You will know you are God. I will know you and you will know me. Having known each other in this violent state by the masks we now wear, we will return to the unity of one made up of others, to be brothers in that heavenly state.

It is Moses who betrays God's name. Now that you know it, ask for wealth in the name of God by saying: "I am wealthy." You cannot point outside of self and call upon God's name. If I am in an impoverished state and desire the state of wealth, I must dare to assume I am wealthy. The Torah is a discussion between Jehovah and Pharaoh, or faith and doubt. You must have the faith of assumption that you are the man you want to be in order to become it. Your desires will never come to pass if you believe the denials displayed by your reason and outer senses. As you walk in the assumption that your desire is fulfilled, you are calling upon the name of God and conjuring that which you are assuming. You must dare to assume wealth, if that is your objective.

If you desire health, you must assume it, even though the doctor's reasoning world produces proof to the contrary. You must be ever aware that they are not your God, that there is only one God and his name is I am! When you point to another as an authority in your world, you are transferring the power that belongs to God to an idol. Now, if you call for anything with the name of God, and his name is I am, and you say I am – are you not your own maker?

God is, for I am! I kill and I make alive, I wound and I heal. I create the light and I form the darkness and besides me there is no other God. Whatever I want, I must assume the full responsibility for it. If I want to conjure health and the doctors tell me I cannot overcome my illness and I believe them, I have made my choice and must accept the responsibility for it. But if I dare to assume health, God is proclaiming it, for he has no name other than I am! This is the grand revelation found in the third chapter, the 14th verse, of Exodus. "Go and tell them `I am has sent me to you.' "Whatever you declare, is; for God's name is any form of the verb to be, whether it is I am, I was, or I will be.

Remember: Moses is not a person, but an eternal plan of God. He was shown everything and told to follow the pattern that he saw in the mountain. No one knows who wrote the books of the Torah. They are only signed with the letters J, B, and P. In fact, we do not know the author of any book in the

Bible. Matthew, Mark, Luke, and John are anonymous names of those who wrote their own visions and revelations of God's eternal plan of salvation. In the state of Moses, I have been leading you into a new and perilous way. I have called you as a group, and explained what has happened to me – the pattern man – in the hope that you will hear me with faith. Not everyone will believe me, just as they did not believe Moses.

It is said that as he led the people through the desert, the majority wanted to go back to their old way of thinking. They felt safer in their old beliefs. It was easier to remain a slave and receive a handout. Many slaves do not want to be freed, because as slaves they are sheltered and fed. To be freed from that state means they would have to enter the state of independence, which is hard but glorious. When you believe God is your own wonderful loving human imagination, you are freed from the slavery of the belief in another. Man has been taught to believe in an external God. To turn to him when in need; and even if he doesn't respond, man continues to think God is doing his work. But Moses tells us to turn to no other God, saying: "Besides me there is no other."

The only God who will bring you out of slavery is I am. While enslaved, assume I am free, and have the courage to continue worshiping the only God, for there is no other. God did not promise life without peril, because you are capable of falling back into your former state of consciousness. Thinking you may have made a mistake, you can again bow before man–made icons and go to mass on Sunday mornings. So, Moses leads you to the promised land, but he cannot take you in. This you must do by yourself. Moses is the pattern in germinal form that erupts as Jesus. When everything said of Jesus Christ in scripture erupts in you, you stand amazed to realize that you are He! That there never was another. That the one and only God and his pattern of salvation, is buried in all humanity.

Now, you either believe my words or you do not. It's entirely up to you. I have told you what I saw on the mountain top – the great Mount Sinai where the laws were given in the beginning. Having experienced that which was seen in the beginning, I have come to tell you, my people, exactly what happened, and I have not altered it. In the state of Moses, I have led you out of the land of Egypt. And when the time for my departure comes, I – a servant of the Lord – will die and be buried by God Himself. This is the great mystery of the seed. Unless it falls into the ground and dies it remains alone, but if it dies it brings forth much. The pattern, like a seed, is planted in the earth, called Adam. The seed will take root and unfold according to its pattern.

The first eruption is to awaken; for just like a seed, the moment a little shoot comes out you know the seed is alive and has taken root. God is a god of the living and not the dead, so what seemingly was dead awakens, and man resurrects within himself. Awakening within your immortal skull where you were buried, you come out and scripture unfolds before you. A child, symbolizing your birth, is present. Three witnesses are there to fulfill scripture. Five months later the pattern erupts again and David stands before you and calls you Father. You will recognize him and proclaim the words of the second Psalm: "Thou art my son, today I have begotten thee."

The relationship between you and your son cannot be described; yet there is no uncertainty as to his identity or yours. The third eruption occurs four months later, when your body is split by a bolt of lightning. (The lovely hymn, "Rock of

Ages," calls it a cleft, saying: "Rock of ages cleft for me.") When your body is cleft, you see golden, liquid light at its base. Fusing with it, you become a coiled, fiery serpent and – like a bolt of lightning – you uncoil right into your skull as it reverberates like thunder. These are the first three acts of the unfolding of God in you. Then, after a period of two years and nine months, the pattern completes itself, as a dove – the symbol of the Holy Spirit – gives his seal of approval by descending and smothering you with affection.

Unable to deny your visions, you will share them with others, cautioning them, telling them that the way is perilous, for you are taking them into a new land. And if they follow you, everyone will have a common experience. Because we all differ, no two will experience the pattern in an identical manner, but everyone will meet David. Regardless of the color of your skin or your gender, you are going to meet a blond, blue–eyed lad who will call you father. David is not looking for a man after the flesh, but the God who is his father, and you will know that you are he! Moses is God's pattern of salvation in germinal form. Having seen the pattern, Moses does not take you into the promised land, but reveals the pattern to you.

It is Joshua who enters and Jesus who unfolds as the pattern within you. If, in the spirit, David calls you My Lord, and scripture tells you that David called Jesus My Lord, are you not Jesus? Are you not he who said: "I am the Lord who brought you out of the land of Egypt, out of the house of bondage?" Perhaps you have a friend who desires to enjoy good health. You can give it to him in the name of God by listening to your thoughts and hearing your friend tell you he has never felt better. Who is hearing the words? I am. That's the Lord. Respond by telling your friend how great he looks in your imagination, and God is speaking. If your friend is unemployed, hear him tell you he now has a wonderful job. Congratulate him and feel the joy that would be yours were it true.

Then ask yourself who is doing it and you, the Lord, will say, I am! All day long man exercises his creative power, unwittingly bringing confusion into his world. Then he rushes to a church and prays to a God who does not exist, for the only God is I am! There is no other God and there never was another God. Practice the law of identical harvest by going to the mountain top. I hope your ambition is to have scripture unfold within you, for that would transcend anything here.

But, perhaps you are one of those who want to leave this world so famous or wealthy that your remains will reside in some huge mausoleum, even though there is no assurance the building and its contents will survive. If so, that's all right, but you now know where Moses is buried. Throughout the centuries men have been looking for Moses in the wrong place. Thinking he was buried on the outside, they search in vain, for God buried him in the skull of man.

Containing God's plan of salvation, Moses reveals the pattern which – when it unfolds – saves man. The word Jesus means, "Jehovah saves". When God's pattern unfolds, God has saved himself. Like a seed which disappears as it becomes what it contained, the pattern unfolds into the tree of life to become one with God, the Father of the seed. Take my message to heart and dwell upon it. Set your mind fully upon this hope that God's pattern of salvation will erupt in you while you are in this sphere. It must erupt for you to leave this world of sin and death and enter eternity. There you will be a king within yourself, creating – not by reason, but by the life you know to be yourself. There you will no longer be an animated body; but as a life–giving spirit, you are God Himself.

When you read scripture in the future, don't think of it as records of myth or secular history, but glorious revelations of God as eternal states of consciousness, personified. Moses is the personification of an eternal state containing the perfect pattern God designed for the purpose of saving himself. It is God who became man that man may become God. Knowing that he had the power to die and overcome death, God died. Now he must overcome death, and he will. History tells us of the great Roman Empire and the Chinese Empire. We are living in the day when the great British Empire is vanishing. There was a time when the sun never set on the British Empire, and now it has diminished in size to almost nothing. Every empire dies in time.

People die and dynasties die and all of the great fortunes will die. I understand that Hughes and Getty both have a personal fortune in excess of one billion dollars. If their fortune was invested at six percent interest, they would receive $175 thousand a day, seven days a week. Yet, when they leave this little segment of time, they will not take it with them. That's this society, so why put your hope in it? Instead, put your hope upon this plan contained in Moses, for buried in you God's plan will erupt and you will enter the promised land as Joshua, called Jesus.

Now let us go into the silence.

Yours *for the* Taking

There is only one cause for the phenomena of life. That cause is God. Housed in you, God is a person in the most literal sense of the word. Believe me, for I know this from experience. God, the only creator, is pure imagination working in the depth of your soul. God began a good work in you and He will bring it to completion on the day God's creative power is unveiled in you! God's creative power and wisdom is defined in scripture as Christ. When Christ unveils himself in you, you will know you are God's power and God's wisdom.

God, your own wonderful human imagination, underlies all of your faculties, including perception, and streams into your surface mind least disguised in the form of creative, productive fantasy. When you ask yourself what you can do to transcend your present limitation of life, you are dwelling upon the means. God does not ask you to consider the means, but to define the end. Speaking to you through the medium of desire, God asks the question: "What wantest thou of me?" Then he tells you not to be concerned with the ways and means, for his ways are unsearchable. They are inscrutable and past finding out. This statement you will find in the 11th chapter of the Book of Romans. So don't be concerned as to how God will fulfill the end, only know that He will. Can you believe your desire is fulfilled? Can you believe it is true? If you can, it is yours for the taking, for nothing is impossible to one who believes.

Now, let me share with you three stories which came to me during the summer. The first letter was from my friend Bennie. In it he told of lying prone on his bed, face down, when he felt as though someone grabbed his shoulders; and as he was lifted up he heard the words: "Take a stand!" Intuitively he knew he had to make the decision now as to whether he was going to believe that imagining creates reality or disbelieve it.

Scripture tells us, "He who is not with me is against me." There is no neutral ground, for "I have not come to bring peace, but a sword. To set a man against his father and a daughter against her mother." Why? Because a man's enemies are within him. Everyone must eventually take the stand that imagining creates reality and swim or sink with this concept.

Now, a few days later while in meditation, Bennie felt himself being held from behind by three men. As they raised him, he watched the sun rise and heard the words: "Look! Behold!" and "Recognition!" And he remembered a passage from my book, Your Faith Is Your Fortune: "Recognition of this truth will transform you from one who tries to make it so, into one who recognizes it to be so."

Soon after this, a friend asked Ben to pray for him. He wanted to be the property manager of the company he worked for. Although he had been passed by year after year, Bennie told him what to do, and imagined hearing the friend tell him the job was now his. A few months later the job was vacated and his friend was given the position with an increase in salary and greater responsibility, just as he had imagined. What did Bennie do? He imagined! To whom did he pray? To his own wonderful human imagination! God, the creator of all life, is like pure imagining in you, underlying all of your faculties - including perception. He streams into your surface mind least disguised in the form of productive fantasy. Bennie took a stand. He prayed for his friend and believed his prayer was answered. He tested himself, and the windows of heaven opened and poured forth blessings for all to see. Now Bennie knows that with God all things are possible.

God is your mightier self. Emptying himself, God took on the form of a slave and is now found in the likeness of man. Abdicating his power, Pure Imagination took upon himself the limitations of flesh, thereby becoming human. It is God who weaves your every desire into cubic reality, waiting upon you effectively and swiftly, regardless of whether your desire is for evil or for good. The one who conjures thoughts in the mind of a Hitler or Stalin is the same power as the one conjuring thoughts in the mind of a pope or the Arch Bishop of Canterbury. There aren't two Gods. There is only one!

The 14th and 53rd chapters of the Book of Psalms are identical, each telling us: "The fool says in his heart there is no God, but the Lord looks down from heaven upon the children of the many to see if there are any that act wise and seek the Lord." Here we find that in the eyes of God, wisdom is equated with seeking the Lord. And if God is all-wise and all powerful, then any search other than for the Lord is stupid. You may be the greatest mathematician or scientist, the most intelligent and honored man among men, but if your search is not for God, you are stupid in His eyes.

Called upon to look for the cause of creation, what are you doing losing yourself in the phenomena of life? When something happens, search your thoughts and you will discover your own wonderful human imagination to be the cause of your experience, because God is a person. At the present time He is wearing a mask called Neville, but the one speaking to you now knows himself to be the Ancient of Days. Every being in the world is a mask worn by God; for housed in man, is man's imagination.

A thought acted upon is an imaginal act. Think (imagine) a horrible earthquake and God will give it to you. Imagine (think of) a war and God will provide that, too. Imagine peace and you will have it. God will give you health if you will but imagine being healthy. Imagine success and you will have it. The moment you think, you are feeding your imagination, which is a person. I use the word person deliberately, for you are a person. You are the mask God is now wearing, for God became you that you may become God.

Now let me share another letter with you. Last year this lady, living about sixty miles north of San Francisco, was possessed with the desire to come to Los Angeles and attend my lecture. Leaving word at her office, she drove her car to the San Francisco airport, where she took a plane to Los Angeles. There she was met by a friend and immediately came to the lecture. After the lecture she joined a group of four women and one man for coffee, where she expressed her hunger, having missed lunch and dinner that day. The gentleman sitting beside her then said, "I'd like to buy you a steak." And as she looked into his face she heard a voice within her say, "This is your husband."

Now, this lady has been married and divorced four times, so she had specific desires for a husband which she felt must be fulfilled. She wanted to be happily married to a man who lived by this truth. She wanted him to love and respect her as well as her seventeen-year-old son. Having imagined such a man in September, she attended my meeting in October, and married the gentleman she met here the following January.

The gentleman added his story to her letter, saying: "Having played with the idea of being married, I went to a pawn shop last September and purchased a plain gold band which I placed on the third finger of my left hand. Every day I wore the ring and every night I slept in the feeling of being happily married. (My friend thought he could not get the feeling of being married without a physical aid, but you don't need anything outside of your imagination to catch the mood.)

Having been an alcoholic, this gentleman imagined his wife never mentioned his past; for although he had not tasted alcohol for nine years, he had paid the price in his search for God. You see, the alcoholic is searching for truth. Thirsty, he finds a false spirit in the form of alcohol, while those who will not touch it - and criticize those who do - haven't even started their search. But I have news for them. One day they, too, will know a hunger which will not be satisfied by bread. They will know a thirst so great they will make the mistake of clothing it in the form of a bottle. But because it will be a false thirst, the thirst will remain. Then they will discover the true hunger and the true thirst, which is for the hearing of the word of God.

Now, in the third letter a gentleman writes: "Having borrowed from the bank, every month when I sent in my payment I reduced the total amount in my record book. One day, as I was writing my check and recording its payment, I closed my eyes and saw two zeros under the balance due column. Then I gave a sigh of relief because the note was paid. For the next three months I persisted in seeing those double zeros and rejoicing in being debt-free. Then came an unexpected surprise! Our company paid us all a mid-year bonus which was so large I was able to pay all of my bills, including the bank loan, and deposit the rest in the bank."

Now I think this gentleman and I must be two peas in the same pod, because money seems to burn in his pocket, too. Instead of keeping the money in the bank as the rational mind would do, my friend began to think about how to spend it, so of course he found a way. He bought a tape recorder to bring and record my message!

To whom did my friend turn when he wanted the bank loan paid? He turned to God! He did not get down on his knees and ask some outside God to do it for him. He didn't go to church and consult a priest, rabbi or minister. He didn't contact a so-called truth teacher, but simply closed his eyes to the obvious and saw two zeros in the balance due column. Then for the first time in the history of his company a mid-year bonus was paid. This happened to him because of his use of the law, and his knowledge of who God is.

Not everyone who seeks God finds him, but there are those - like Philip -that when they find him, they bring their brother Nathanael. Andrew found Jesus and brought Peter. You, too, will find Jesus when you exercise your imagination, and bring those you love to his awareness. If great wealth befell you, would not your wife (or husband), your children, as well as those in your immediate circle benefit from your good fortune? And if it befell them, would it not befall you? So, we benefit each other as we search out God and test him.

Revelation tells us to be either hot or cold, but never to be lukewarm. If you do not believe me to the point of testing the law, you are lukewarm. But one day, like Ben, you will take a stand. You will either be for me or against me. You will try to believe that imagining creates reality, or reject it. You will be hot or cold about it, and that is better than being lukewarm. I have discovered that those who hated me at first when I took from them their idols, the icon in their mind called Jesus, have become my finest students. So many people claim they believe in Jesus, but cannot define him. Unable to place him in time and space, they are defiant when I say: Christ in you is your hope of glory. Full of insults, they are cold. Some have even been violent. But one day they will find him of whom Moses and the prophets wrote, turn around, and be embraced by the Lord.

I started telling this story in the 1930's and here we are in the 1960's. During these thirty-odd years I have found those who really opposed me - those who were so moved and disturbed they were determined to disprove my words. But since they couldn't do it, they too have found God to be their own wonderful human imagination. The Bible is addressed only to the human imagination. In Blake's famous letter to the Rev. Dr. Trusler he makes this comment: "Why is the Bible more entertaining and instructive than any other book? Is it not because it is addressed to the imagination, which is spiritual sensation, and only immediately to the understanding, or reason?"

The Bible is imaginative instruction. When it unfolds in you it is more real than anything here, yet it is all imagined, for God is all imagination and so is man. The eternal body of man is the imagination, and that is God Himself. There is nothing but this one body called Jesus, who is the Lord God Jehovah.

I tell you, God became as we are that we may become as He is. No one took God's life. He laid it down himself saying: "I have the power to lay it down and the power to lift it up again. The fall into fragmented space was deliberate. And He who fell has the power to gather us all together, one by one, into that single body who is all love. His body is above the organization of sex. In it there is no Greek, no Jew, no bond, no free, no male, no female. When you wear it you understand Paul's statement: "I consider the sufferings of this present time not worth comparing to the glory that has been revealed in me." In that body you know yourself to be the real Man, and this fleshly body as nothing. You will realize that you were never male or female, but have always been God.

Remember, everything is yours for the taking. If you want it, take it. If you cannot claim it for yourself, ask a friend for help. If you want to be happily married, do what my friends did. You want to pay off all of your debts? Whatever you desire is yours. All you have to do is imagine you have it, for everything in life is yours for the taking!

Now let us go into the silence.

www.ingramcontent.com/pod-product-compliance
Lightning Source LLC
Chambersburg PA
CBHW021134020426
42331CB00005B/776